HOW TO
RECYCLE BUILDINGS

LAURENCE E. REINER, M.E., P.E.

THE McGRAW-HILL BOOK COMPANY

NEW YORK   ST. LOUIS   SAN FRANCISCO   AUCKLAND   BOGOTÁ

DÜSSELDORF   JOHANNESBURG   LONDON   MADRID   MEXICO

MONTREAL   NEW DELHI   PANAMA   PARIS   SÃO PAULO

SINGAPORE   SYDNEY   TOKYO   TORONTO

Library of Congress Cataloging in Publication Data

Reiner, Laurence E
    How to recycle buildings.

    Includes index.
    1. Buildings—Repair and reconstruction.   2. Build-
ings—Remodeling for other use.   I. Title.
TH3401.R44   690′.24   79-13633
ISBN 0-07-051840-8

1234567890   BPBP   7865432109

The editors for this book were Jeremy Robinson and Elizabeth P. Richardson,
the designer was William Frost, and the production supervisor
was Sally Fliess. It was set in Melior
by University Graphics, Inc.

Printed and bound by The Book Press.

CONTENTS

19 Case Study Three: The Ironfronts, Richmond, Virginia 183

20 Case Study Four: Weyerbacher Terrace, Indianapolis, Indiana 209

PREFACE

Probably the most neglected resource of this country is its stock of old buildings. There are many thousands of these buildings in our cities and older suburban communities. Many of these structures were built before the turn of the century, and they were built to last. There are warehouses, railroad stations, factories, row houses, apartment houses, hospitals, and even more recently built service stations and supermarkets. They are there because progress or economics has passed them by or made them unprofitable to operate in their present condition. The shoe factory has closed because imported shoes are cheaper, the cotton mill has closed because the textile industry has moved away, and the loft building has closed because labor is cheaper elsewhere.

There is another important reason for the abandonment or underutilization of inner-city structures. During the past several decades there has been a constant migration to the cities of the poor and the disadvantaged. These people pay little or nothing in taxes and require expensive services. As most of a city's revenue comes from property taxes, the resultant heavy taxes on middle-income property owners has resulted in a flight to the suburbs. These families have taken with them various support services such as retail centers, light manufacturing, and office building users.

Cities are very conscious of this loss of revenue, and many are in serious financial difficulties because of it. The city in its desire to reverse the trend, to attract middle-income tax-paying families back, is faced with a dilemma. It cannot subsidize recycling of old buildings for new uses or for the building's original use without being accused of favoring "the rich" or of threatening a low-rent neighborhood by an influx of new more expensive housing. No city has yet made any significant move toward any form of tax relief or zoning relief for recycling. At present the city is neutral, but the time is closely approaching when the city must move positively toward helping the recycling entrepreneur if only to save itself.

The resurrection of these old buildings is one of the great hopes for the future of architecture and construction in this country. It is becoming more apparent every day that the trend toward the recycling of these buildings is becoming stronger. It can be said that in this country, whose resources have now been shown to be limited, it is becoming the fashionable thing to do. Many in the real estate, design, and construction professions have hesitated to become involved in this business because they may view it as "alteration" work, but this is not so. These buildings are waiting for the skilled, imaginative hand of the architect, the intelligent developer and the engineer to give them new life.

While the recycling process in this country is still in its infancy, it is taking hold. During the past several years the recycling and the rejuvenation of buildings of all sorts has become an important factor in the architectural profession and in the construction industry. The general public has become conscious of the tremendous waste that occurs when an old building is destroyed and the space it occupied becomes another parking lot or just an abandoned lot. The practicality of recycling is never more apparent than in marginal areas where the excessive cost of new construction is not justified but a recycling project may very well be.

The federal government has increasingly become aware of the value of older buildings and the advantages of recycling. New laws have been passed which set aside increased money for funding National Historic Preservation and which grant new tax advantages to recycle buildings that fall under this category. Many towns throughout the country have become aware of their Main Streets, which in many cases have been allowed to fall into a state of disrepair and have lost business to the glittering new shopping centers. Encouraged by the town fathers and with financing made available, architects have undertaken a complete rejuvenation of many of the structures on such streets. The purpose can be twofold: (1) such a rejuvenation restores the historical architecture of the street, and (2) such projects can be made to pay their own way and more. It is of course not practical to try to use such a project for a supermarket or any other venture that would directly compete with the shopping center, but it can become a boutique, a bookstore, a cocktail lounge, etc., and the restored upper floors can be rented for all sorts of office use. This kind of recycling is not limited to smaller cities or towns. Large city neighborhoods which have gone downhill are also being looked at.

Major downtown renewals, which are multimillion-dollar projects and require major government and private financing, are in another category. These large downtown renewals may very well create fringe areas which can be rewarding for the smaller entrepreneur. This book confines itself to the smaller individual project and does not discuss major renewals.

It must be understood, of course, that not every old building can be recycled for a useful purpose or for the purpose that it may seem best suited for. A mill building that would make an excellent office building cannot be recycled for this purpose if the present office buildings in the town are partly empty and have lowered their rents. There is no reason, however, why this building cannot be turned into a modern factory or assembly plant with a brightly painted interior and good lighting and with stairways and electrical and sanitary facilities in compliance with the present code.

Many of these old buildings are still in the hands of the original owners or their heirs or in a trust, or they may be owned by a charitable or educational institution. They are not abandoned, but neither are they profitable. Many of these buildings are in neighborhoods which, once left behind by progress, are now, because of economic pressures, beginning to revive. The alert real estate consultant in combination with an architect and an engineer can approach such owners with his suggestions for a profitable solution for these problem buildings. It will take time on the part of all of these professionals to conduct a proper study, but it can be repaid many times over by the commissions that may ensue. And the news of successful building recyclings travels fast.

The profitable recycling of a building—and it must be profitable if the recycling process is to be continued—requires imagination, know-how, and the courage to speculate. A great deal of the speculative risk can be removed by intelligent forward planning and by following a step-by-step procedure that will assure a lending institution that everything that can be done has been done by the architect, the engineer, and the developer to make the project a success.

Some recycling projects involve no speculative risk at all. An example would be a manufacturer who has outgrown his present plant and who purchases an existing building and restructures it for his own use. On some occasions a real estate consultant or an architect may be given a commission to find an old building and to recycle it for the specific use of the sponsor.

In such cases even if the speculative risk is removed, the step-by-step process must still be gone through if the resultant building is to successfully serve the purpose for which it was recycled. The proper location must be found; the soundness of the building must be established; its structural characteristics such as floor heights, floor areas, column spacing, etc., must be at least reasonably compatible for its new use. And the new plan must meet building codes, zoning codes, the OSHA code, and the new parameters for the conservation of energy. In other words the only difference between a commissioned recycling and one with some elements of speculation in it is the absence of the speculative risk and in the financing.

There are many instances of the recycling of structures for private residential use. Such projects have gained wide publicity in house-oriented magazines and architectural publications. To a great extent the finished product is used by the person who has performed the recycling. There are instances in which a chicken coop, a power house, an old loft building, a railroad station, and many other unlikely structures have been changed for residential use. Such personal projects, however, will not be considered in this book. The purpose of this book is to set forth in complete detail the knowledge that is necessary for a profitable and commercially sound recycling.

As we have mentioned, many architects, builders, and entrepreneurs avoid recycling because it is considered an "alteration" and gives no play to creative skills. Another reason is the possibility of heavy cost overruns which can occur in such work. This fear can be overcome by a study of the developing techniques of recycling. Tightly drawn plans and specifications which exactly delineate the work to be done will calm the general contractor's (and the subcontractor's) fears and cause him to prepare a tight, competitive bid. An informed source has described recycling as "the development path of least resistance. It can be predictable, competitive, profitable, and manageable."

It is the author's opinion, shared by many architects, engineers, real estate people, and building contractors, that recycling is here to stay and to expand. It is an answer to the high cost of new construction; it is a saver of scarce resources; it is a saver of time; it is a saver of energy; and it is profitable for all concerned.

The use of the masculine pronoun in this book should be taken in a purely generic sense, in no way meant to deny the role women already play in architecture and construction or their increasing importance in the field of recycling. "He" and "his" have been employed solely to avoid the grammatical awkwardness of the "he or she" or "his/her" types of phrasing.

LAURENCE E. REINER

1

A MARKETING

SURVEY

1-1 THE PURPOSE OF THE SURVEY

The architect, developer, builder, or entrepreneur who wishes to become involved in rejuvenating and restructuring a building must first make sure that the finished product will serve a need of the market (whether expressed or latent), that it will be completely useful for its new purpose, and that it will be competitively priced. The purpose of the marketing survey is therefore to determine the best and most profitable use of an old or disused structure consistent with the needs of the area for shelter for people, business, government, or institutional or other uses.

Marketing can be defined as the performance of all the necessary activities for determining the needs and wants of markets. In the proposed recycling of a building, the primary function of a marketing survey is to gather information that will lead to a finished product for which there is a need. In the recycling process a building is acquired; it is turned into a more useful form; it is promoted (marketed); and it is consumed. The consumer may be an individual, a business (used in its widest sense), an arm of government, or an institution.

Such a survey is necessary even when there is a sponsor, e.g., manufacturer or any business which requires larger and more modern facilities. The enterprise commissioning the recycling of an old building will be unhappy if the final price is more than the budget allowed, if the final facility is unsatisfactory, or if the general feeling is that they would have done better by constructing an entirely new building.

The marketing survey has another very important purpose. After the survey has determined the most profitable new use for an old building, it becomes necessary to convince a lending institution, an individual, a group, or any other source of funds that the recycling will be useful. The lender must be assured that the loan will be repaid with enough profit to justify the risk capital involved.

1-2   THE GROWTH OF THE AREA AND THE COMMUNITY

It should not be necessary for the real estate consultant, the architect, or others who undertake a recycling project to make a detailed survey of the economic health of the area. The parties involved should be aware of the general growth of the area and of the community. To supplement this knowledge there are census reports, marketing surveys, real estate periodicals, and trade papers in libraries or at chambers of commerce or real estate boards. And of course there are the real estate and financial sections of all city and community newspapers and magazines.

A sample tabulation of what an area survey might look like is shown in Table 1-1. It is a survey of an area containing small cities and towns within commuting distance of a large regional center. This is a fairly prosperous high-income area, but there are many excellent and stable areas where the median income is lower and there may not be any institutions of higher learning or as many banks. There have been successful recyclings in towns of 20,000 or less located in such areas.

Big cities and metropolitan areas have rules of their own. It is best in such cases to make a survey by individual communities or neighborhoods, always keeping in mind the stability of the entire city. The same format can be used with some modification. The tabulation will be helpful in focusing the entire situation.

In recycling, however, the growth and economic strength of a community are not as important as they would be for new construction. Buildings that present good prospects for successful modernization are not usually in areas where new construction would be considered, and

TABLE 1-1   TYPICAL AREA SURVEY

James County, 626 mi^2

Item	Maximum points	Rating
Population growth:		
653,000 (1960)		
792,000 (1970) +21%		
819,000 (1973) +3.4%	10	8
Population aged 19–49:		
198,000 24%	5	3
Median family income:		
$12,086	10	7
Institutional influence:		
2 universities, 1 community college (22,300 students)	5	3
Governmental activities:		
None	5	0
Marketing and retail centers:		
2 towns and retail centers	5	3
Transportation:		
1 main line, 2 spurs, 1 north-south expressway, 1 secondary airport, 40 min to major airport	5	4
Industry and employment:		
Aircraft, machine tools employ 91,000; total employment 260,000	10	8
Bedroom communities:		
Several around city X and city Y; employment out of county 30,000; majority well paid	10	7
Agriculture:		
Dairy and truck farms	5	1
Banks and branches:		
170 including buildings and loans	5	5
Dwelling units:		
154,000 (1950)		
209,000 (1960)		
254,000 (1970)		
+21.8% from 1960	10	9
Movement in or out of industry:		
Movement in from nearby large population center	10	7
Contractor's judgment of overall economic stability	5	5

they appeal to a different need. A city may be stable or even in a slight decline and a well-thought-out recycling job will still be highly successful. A row of old warehouses or abandoned produce markets located a short walk from a downtown business center can be changed into a row of town houses or efficiency apartments successfully. Such a project can fulfill a need that may have been latent until it was conceived and promoted.

Many very successful recycling projects have been conceived and completed where at first glance the areas and buildings seem unsuitable for the purpose. An example is an abandoned hospital in a somewhat run-down neighborhood that was recycled for use as an apartment building. It took imagination and ingenuity, and the result is an example of excellent architectural thinking (see Chap. 20).

1-3   DETERMINING THE NEEDS OF THE COMMUNITY

The question immediately arises: How should this be accomplished? Does the entrepreneur look for old buildings in general? Does he first determine what the community needs and then look for specific buildings? Does he approach owners of problem buildings to offer his services? Which comes first?

The best answer lies in a combination. The entrepreneur can make a survey of the kind of use that will best fill a requirement. At the same time he can make a survey of buildings with a view to determining which building will best serve such a requirement.

Office Building

In general the conversion to an office building can be the most profitable. Office buildings command higher rents than almost any other type of occupancy. They require less plumbing, less partitioning, and fewer facilities than a multifamily use and are easier to manage. An office building can be used by professionals, business, or government.

A survey of the needs for such a use would go through the following steps:

A study of all the existing office buildings in town and in the surrounding area to ascertain their percentage of occupancy, a list of the tenants, and their rental rate

An enquiry among all real estate brokers and management firms regarding need for office space at less than the prevailing downtown rates but in buildings that are not in a 100 percent area

A visit to the chamber of commerce to check the movement of any enterprise into the vicinity

A study of the older or unfashionable neighborhoods to determine whether there has been any movement of new offices into the area

A study of any trade papers to check details of new leases, expansion of space, etc.

A study of government offices (city, county, state, or federal) to determine whether any expansion is needed or is contemplated (lease terms are public information)

The information gathered from this survey should tell whether there is a need for office space in an area somewhat remote from "downtown" and the rental rate which will be competitive enough to lure tenants away from downtown buildings.

Apartment Building or Condominium

In a number of successful recycling projects abandoned loft buildings, warehouses, run-down town houses, or residential buildings have been turned into modern apartments or condominiums. There is really no set rule for determining the need, which is often not expressed. The usual middle-income apartment dweller or condominium purchaser does not rent or buy through an agent, and a survey of existing multifamily dwellings will not tell very much.

What can be done is to study advertisements for rental apartments and condominiums and to speak to janitors or caretakers, etc., of apartment buildings to find out about occupancy and rental rates. Another way of determining the need (if the businesses allow it) is to post a notice on an employee board that asks several questions: Would you like to live within walking distance of your job? What would you consider a reasonable per room monthly rental for an apartment? Would you be interested in the purchase of a condominium apartment? There could be a number of stamped addressed post cards for the answers. A few hundred cards in various locations should give an idea of what is wanted. "Walking distance" can be up to ½ mi.

Above all it requires imagination. A seacoast town had several large partially abandoned boarding houses across a wide waterfront street from fishing-boat docks and coastal steamer docks. They had a view of the water and a distant shore but were abandoned because boat traffic had almost disappeared. They were only six or seven blocks from the downtown area. The interior of each building was gutted and recycled into four or five modern apartments. In this metropolitan area of 100,000 people the apartments were all taken before they were completed. The owners are earning considerably more than 15 percent on their invested capital.

Government Activities

What activity of government can be housed advantageously in a recycled building, and how much recycling must be done to satisfy this activity? If it is an office activity, it must be an office building. But it may be an operation that requires a lot of space but only a few people, such as a computer center, or large areas for mass filing and a combination library and bookstore for government publications. Since such activities do not pay a high rent, not much has to be done to house them. Sanitary facilities, fireproof exits to comply with the codes, painting, lighting, and minimal air conditioning and heating are often sufficient (except for a computer center).

Nursing or Convalescent Home

A number of apartment houses and other suitable buildings have been recycled to serve as nursing or convalescent homes. Such an extremely specialized operation should not be attempted unless there is a sponsor with sufficient financial capacity to carry it to a successful conclusion.

The recycling team in this case must constantly consult with the proper authorities to be sure that the necessary licenses will be issued and that the project will be designed so that it will qualify for top government aid. Authority must be brought in from the very beginning and before a definite site is chosen.

Factory

An abandoned or underutilized factory building or warehouse might be considered for recycling into a modern manufacturing plant for making anything from clothing to plastics. Such structures are likely to be farther removed from the city or town centers than buildings to be used for other purposes, but they are also likely, in consequence, to be more reasonably priced.

A survey of real estate brokers dealing in industrial rentals can be made. A survey can also be made of existing smaller industrial operations to determine whether any of them has need for expansion and to find the scale of rent they are willing to pay.

In looking for a building for such a purpose the entrepreneur must remember that a building suitable for clothing manufacture may not be suitable for paint or plastic manufacture. The fire and building codes must be carefully investigated before any commitment is made.

Other Uses

The right kind of structure can be recycled to meet as many uses as any new building can. It can be changed into a combination warehouse and showroom, a merchandise exchange, an antique exchange, a laboratory, a neighborhood center for nonprofit activities, or a child-care center.

Newer Buildings

Successful recycling need not start with an old building. In any number of cases a comparatively new multifamily dwelling has been changed into an office building, or conversely an office building has been converted into a multifamily dwelling. These structures are almost always located in good areas of mixed higher residential and commercial use. The reasons for their conversion can be quite simple, e.g., an owner's quest for a higher profit, which can only be obtained from a new use. If a building was built for a certain use which did not develop, it must be changed to another function which will be successful. A high-rise condominium which has been changed to a hotel or a school house to a multifamily dwelling are among some of the recyclings that are being done or are contemplated. In such instances a marketing survey must be made to assure that the new use will be successful, even if the areas are stable or on the rise.

It requires a skilled entrepreneur to interpret the needs of a community through marketing research, whether he is a real estate developer, a real estate consultant, a real estate broker, or an architect and engineer team.

1-4   THE ROLE OF THE VARIOUS PARTICIPANTS IN A SURVEY

The real estate developer, the broker, or the consultant will all find the foregoing points on how to make a marketing survey familiar. To an extent this is the kind of survey he must often make for himself or his clients. However, although this may be unfamiliar territory for the architect or the builder, a recycling project need not be started by professional real estate people. There is no reason why it cannot be started by an architect or builder who can then enlist the support of other professionals.

Architect

The architect is well fitted to become the principal in a recycling project. He is a planner and a designer. He can see the possibilities of the redesign of a building facade or a new use for an interior. He is familiar with zoning and building codes and their interpretation. He knows the techniques of construction and should be familiar with the best methods and materials of construction and with newest approved materials.

He is not normally an expert in marketing research, the marketing of a recycling project, construction management, building management, or financing a project. For these matters he can enlist the support of others who are familiar in these fields or he can learn to do them himself. Many highly successful architects are also successful businessmen and real estate experts.

Builder

Marketing surveys are not new to the speculative builder since in the course of his business he must make such surveys in order to assure himself that his speculative venture will be rented or sold. Recycling presents a new challenge for the builder who wishes to diversify from new high-cost construction. The rules for a market survey for a recycle are different, however, from those for such a survey for new construction. The neighborhood is different, the rent scale is different, and usually the clientele is different.

Nevertheless the builder is very well suited to promote a recycling project because of his knowledge of construction costs and materials. He also has a knowledge of zoning and building codes and is familiar with the process of financing a venture. Many medium-sized builders have been very successful in the recycling business.

2

SURVEY OF

NEIGHBORHOODS

2-1 A COMPREHENSIVE VIEW

The next step after the market survey should be a survey of neighborhoods to find where a project would be most attractive to that segment of the market the promoter wishes to attract. Even if he has been commissioned to find a property to serve some definite purpose, he must still find the neighborhood in which this use will best be served.

In many cases architects who have shown an interest in the reconstruction and the recycling of structures are approached by real estate promoters or real estate brokers with a definite property in mind. In these instances the architect may be expected to take a financial interest in the project, at least to the extent of his fee. This can represent a considerable amount of out-of-pocket cost. The architect in partnership with others or by himself must ascertain that the project will be sound both architecturally and financially before he commits himself. All such projects require outside financing, and the architect plays a major part in the development of a sound project. The neighborhood in which the project is located also plays a very important role. Financial institutions are extremely careful in lending construction money in certain areas, and the location of these areas must be ascertained.

It should be made clear at this point that this book is concerned only with the social aspects of recycling insofar as a successful recycling project may help to stabilize a neighborhood. It does not advocate the location or any such project, no matter what its future purpose, in a decaying area where there may be danger to the future occupants or danger of vandalism to the property. Recycling in such an area can be accomplished only with governmental or institutional sponsorship.

Cities and towns have many neighborhoods devoted to residential purposes; others are used for light manufacturing, light warehousing, and service industries. Many neighborhoods are composed of a mixture, with light commercial or retail business infringing upon residential use. There are other areas with decay creeping in. The entrepreneur must be aware of what use or prospect of use is in the ascendancy before he commits time and money to making a detailed survey of that particular neighborhood.

Determination of the Trend

Is the neighborhood stable? Is it deteriorating, or is it being used for new purposes which may start it on an up trend? Remember that the first objective of any proposed recycling is to purchase the property at a price which when added to the reconstruction cost will produce a total cost considerably less than that of a new structure. This will enable the entrepreneur to charge rentals which are below the going market rate in prime locations but will still produce a handsome profit. Where is such a structure to be found? The obvious answer is in an older neighborhood which has been bypassed by progress but which is still stable and being infiltrated by new uses. It is in such neighborhoods that an old factory, an occupied but partly run-down apartment building, an abandoned or partly used warehouse, or a row of narrow-fronted private residences can be found. How does one determine that the neighborhood is stable, will continue to be stable, and will not suddenly start on a downward slide which will leave the entrepreneur high and dry?

USE OF A ZONING MAP

The first step in such a determination is the careful study of a zoning map and the zoning code. There are more than 250 significant metropolitan areas in this country, and of these there are more than 30 with a population of over 1 million. Any one of these 250 places would be a good place to start. There are also many smaller cities and large towns that are ripe for a recycling project. For the moment, however, we shall confine ourselves to the larger metropolitan areas.

The area chosen for the first example is a large north central city. Let us assume that the promoter is familiar with the city in general but not with the character of the many neighborhoods that make up the city. In this case he has no special commission to look for a specific use and is willing to recycle any suitable structure to any use that will have a stabilizing effect on the neighborhood and be profitable. The steps to be followed are the same as if he were working on a specific commission or looking at a property called to his attention. The only difference is that in that case he would be looking at a single neighborhood instead of many.

The master zoning map of this particular city is divided into a grid consisting of mile-square sections. The city has a major downtown business center, which is zoned for high floor-area ratios, thus allowing the high-rise business structures which form the center of office activity. In many smaller subsidiary centers one finds shopping and repair facilities for local residents and also smaller buildings to be used for a variety of allowed uses. These facilities provide a certain amount of local employment. This kind of neighborhood is likely to be stable and to contain a number of structures that are underutilized at any given time. A look at the zoning map shows a number of such mile-square sections which even a cursory knowledge of the city would indicate as stable and reasonably free from creeping decay for the foreseeable future.

The first section considered here is about 1½ mi from the business center (see Fig. 2-1). The zoning map shows a mixture of uses. Medium-density housing is interspersed with light manufacturing, retailing and servicing, including garages, dry-cleaning plants, showrooms, light warehousing, car rentals, machine repair, etc. The map also shows two areas which are set aside for planned residential development. This can be a danger signal, as such planned developments are usually located in deteriorated slum areas. While the area seems to be of the kind in which a property could be purchased at a reasonable price for recycling, it requires almost a street-by-street inspection.

The next section that could be considered, 1 mi farther from the central city (see Fig. 2-2), is of the same mixed use with high- and medium-density residential mixed with various business and high industrial uses. There are no planned developments, and although the schools are fewer, they show much more ground area, which may indicate that they are newer.

Of the 200 or more mile-square sections shown on the zoning map

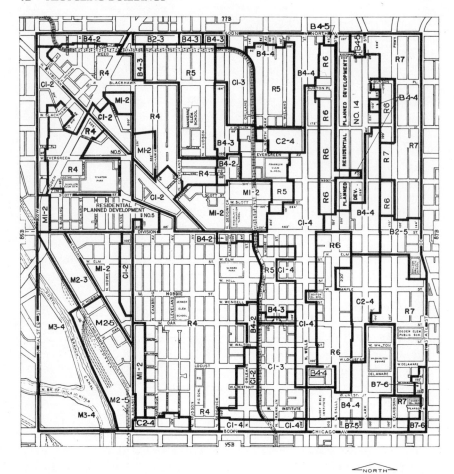

FIGURE 2-1 Zoning map for first section. R1 and R2 = single-family residence district; R3 to R8 = general residence district; B1-1 to B1-5 = local retail districts; B2-1 to B2-5 = restricted retail districts; B3-1 to B3-5 = general retail districts; B4-1 to B4-5 = restricted service districts; B5-1 to B5-5 = general service districts; B6-6 and B6-7 = restricted central business districts; B7-5 to B7-7 = general central business districts; C1-1 to C1-5 = restricted commercial district; C2-1 to C2-5 = general commercial districts; C3-5 to C3-7 = commercial manufacturing districts; C4 = motor freight terminal district; M1-1 to M1-5 = restricted manufacturing district; M2-1 to M2-5 = general manufacturing district; and M3-1 to M3-5 = heavy manufacturing district.

at least 20 sections show an allowed mixture of residential, business, servicing, and light industrial use in the proportion that seems most appropriate for recycling for business or residential use.

It must be emphasized that this close study of a zoning map is essential as a first step without regard to how or if a specific recycling project has been brought to the attention of the entrepreneur.

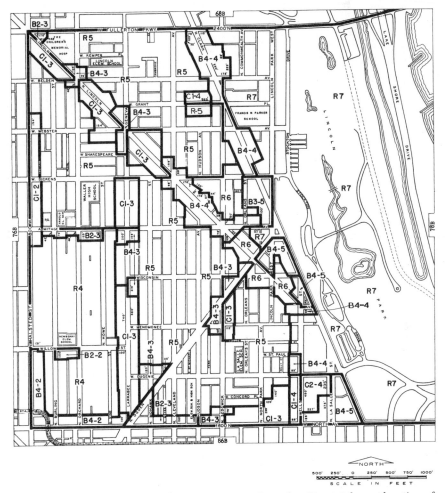

FIGURE 2-2 Zoning map for second section; see legend to Fig. 2-1 for explanation of zoning code.

PHYSICAL INSPECTION OF A NEIGHBORHOOD

The zoning map shows the uses that are allowed, but a physical inspection will show how the neighborhood lives and what sort of people live there. As you walk or drive through the streets, you should look for many things. One of the most important is the use of the sidewalks. Is there a constant movement of people? Do you feel menaced when walking the streets? Do the passersby look alert and purposeful? How are they dressed? Are children playing? In the retail streets are many shops abandoned? Are there many boarded-up or derelict buildings? Are there any signs of new uses for old buildings or shops, a new boutique, beauty parlor, or bar, a reconstructed or freshly painted residence or business building?

The zoning map may show large areas taken up by parks or a hospital complex or a river or railroad tracks and railroad yards (see Fig. 2-3). These are border areas which do not allow through pedestrian or automobile traffic. Such areas are often surrounded by quiet, lonely streets with no retail activity or many passersby. They can be considered dead-end areas. In these times when a lonely area in any town or city is not really safe after dark the recycled apartment or business building that is located near such fringe areas may meet tenant resistance.

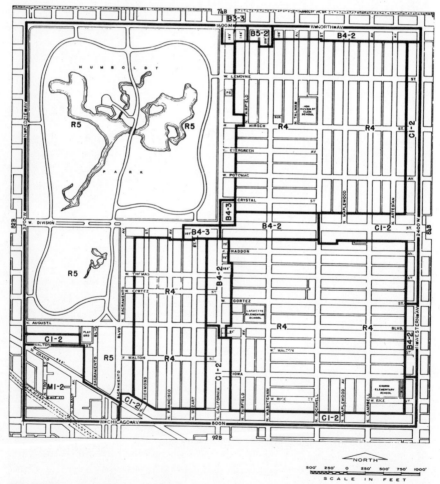

FIGURE 2-3 Zoning map for third section; see legend to Fig. 2-1 for explanation of zoning code.

FIGURE 2-4 This brick building on a busy corner in a business district is for sale.

Another important point in the survey of a neighborhood is the inspection of the surrounding areas to look for any signs of encroaching decay. One must look for abandoned buildings or retail establishments and the physical state of the buildings that are occupied. Is there evidence of poor rubbish collection, abandoned cars in the streets, empty lots that are filled with trash? Would one feel safe on the streets

FIGURE 2-5 This building just around the corner from a busy thoroughfare is being recycled into six apartments.

FIGURE 2-6 Two buildings in good areas ready for recycling.

FIGURE 2-7 Once a gas station, this building now houses a veterinary hospital.

after dark? Creeping decay is caused by many factors beyond the ability of any single entrepreneur to cure or to stop no matter what the object of a recycling job is. Financing is difficult to obtain in areas which seem to be in the path of such decay. It is best to avoid them. If the neighborhood being considered seems to be a good one for a recycling project, the surrounding areas should preferably be similar or better.

2-2   VIABILITY OF A NEIGHBORHOOD

After it has been established that a neighborhood is stable and safe and free from any infringing decay, the next step is to determine what amenities it offers. Whether the object of the recycling is to provide housing or office space or any commercial use, certain matters must be determined.

Transportation

If the proposed project is residential, how are the tenants going to get to work? The survey must look for public transportation first (bus lines, subways, or even a railroad commuter line that may have a station in the area). If such transportation is not immediately available, the private automobile must be used. Would the residential tenants be able to park nearby?

Another answer to the transportation problem is walking. Are there nearby places of employment from which the promoter can hope to attract tenants? The answer can be obtained by the distribution of circulars among the employees. The employer should be pleased to help locate his workers within walking distance.

If the project is to be an office building, a factory, or other commercial venture, how are the employees going to get to work? Again public transportation must be investigated, and the best way to do this is to obtain a comprehensive transportation map of the entire metropolitan area. Such matters as transfer points and double fares should be investigated.

Again if no reasonable public transportation is available, parking space should be provided.

Shopping and Eating

No matter what the project is to be, there should be some neighborhood shopping available. Apartments require groceries, meat and vegetables, drug stores, and shops in which some clothing is available. Offices require some clothing or lingerie shops and at least one food store which can be used at noon or on the way home.

Offices or any commercial venture also require facilities for eating lunch or for send-in coffee or lunch. Many neighborhoods contain luncheonettes and small reasonably priced ethnic restaurants which are popular for lunch and dinner for the local residents.

Schools and Libraries

Most recycled residential projects do not attract families with school-age children, but if a project contains apartments with two bedrooms, it is a distinct possibility that there may be children. In this case a school and library within walking distance are a definite plus. It is not expected that there will be many cultural amenities near a section where a recycling project will be undertaken. The local movie house or library or park may be some distance away, but this need not detract from the success of a project.

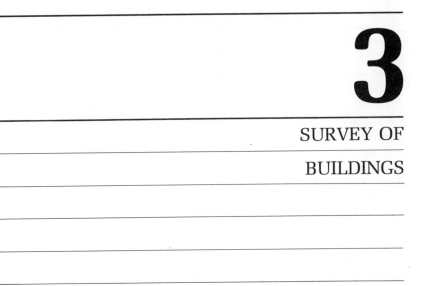

3

SURVEY OF

BUILDINGS

3-1 HOW THE FINAL USE IS DETERMINED

There are several ways to approach this most important objective. If the principal has no specific final use in mind, he can cast a wide net. Experience in the recycling field has shown that some very unlikely buildings have lent themselves to uses which were not apparent to any but the most discerning eye. An old abandoned school is now an art center used for studios and exhibits; a downtown hospital has become an apartment house; a brewery has become an office and apartment complex; and a garage building has become an art center.

If the promoter has made a market survey of the area in order to identify its needs, he should bear in mind that the final use must be in concurrence with these needs but that is the only curb on his imagination.

An architect or real estate consultant is often approached by the owner of a property that has outlived its original purpose because of the obsolescence of its equipment (such as a hospital). A school building may have been replaced by a newer district school, or it may have been abandoned because the school population moved away. Such buildings are likely to be structurally sound and may very well be recycled for completely different purposes. No matter what kind of structure is involved, its final use must be determined by the requirements of the community and by surveys of the physical conditions and adaptability of the buildings and the trends of the neighborhood.

In some cases an architect, a real estate consultant, or a builder may be approached by a principal who is thinking of a recycled building for investment. Or it may be a business enterprise which for various reasons requires larger quarters or a different location.

In all of these cases the principal is motivated toward a recycling because he wishes to avoid the high cost of land, the time and money spent in possible demolition, the high cost of new construction, and the time that must be spent in planning and constructing a new building. In such cases the professional need only find a building in a neighborhood which will best suit the principal's requirements.

3-2   HOW TO FIND THE RIGHT BUILDING

If the searcher has a definite use in mind, how does he find the right building and the location that will best suit the use? After making several neighborhood surveys he will know which neighborhood to study for possibilities. A street-by-street walk through the area is the first step.

The Exterior

The front elevation may be the only view of the building that can be seen at first glance. This is what the prospective housing or office building tenant will see. The discerning eye should be able to see what these people will see and determine whether it will be pleasing to them. Most buildings that are ready for commercial recycling are just buildings. Except in very rare cases they are architecture only insofar as an architect has drawn the original plans; they are not architecture in its definition as "a style or special manner of building." The first decision is whether to attempt to give the building a new facade, which can be very expensive and can clash with the old surrounding buildings even when skillfully done. Many successful recyclings have not attempted to alter the exterior elevations other than to repair the masonry, the fenestration, or other structural material and to paint where necessary to freshen up and preserve them. The best advice seems to be to leave them as they are. Many tenants boast about being in a recycled building. Like recycled paper, smaller cars, or turned-down thermostats, it is becoming a life style.

Up to this point there has only been a discussion of a building exterior when the objective has been an apartment or office building. There are, of course, many other objectives for recycling, and usually, except for the maintenance involved, the material or architectural style of the exterior is of small consequence. This applies to any specialized use which does not involve visiting by the general public. Some examples would be a computer center, a laboratory, a filing center, a distribution center, etc.

It is a different matter when there is a specific commission by a sponsor. This sponsor may wish to display a modern look to his clientele, tenants, or employees. But even in this case the architect may be able to adapt the existing exterior without the expense of doing it over completely, especially if the exterior is in reasonably good shape and was well designed in the first place.

A street-by-street inspection made by someone with a discerning and educated eye is an essential requisite of the selection process.

The Interior

When a building seems by size, location, and exterior condition to fit the requirements set by either the principal or a sponsor, the next step is to inspect the condition of the interior. At first this can be done in a cursory manner with a checklist somewhat as follows:

Type of construction:
    Wall bearing, structural iron, structural steel
    Foundation walls
    Floors and ceilings
    Roof, parapets, and cornices
    Fenestration

Condition:
    Heating and plumbing
    Electrical
    Means of egress (stairs, doors)
    Elevators and shaftways
    General feeling about the state of repair

Adaptability of the Building to a New Use

There is more to an interior inspection than a survey of its structural and mechanical components. The floor heights, column spacing, stairways, and fenestration must be adaptable for the contemplated final use. If a change into an apartment house is contemplated, high ceilings may necessitate a hung ceiling and extra-high fire-resistant partitions. The column spacing may not lend itself to any practical apartment layout. If the building is bounded by a party wall on either side, it may be difficult to use the windowless inner space for human habitation. The building may have possibilities only as an office building, a light-manufacturing loft, or other commercial purpose. If it is not viable as an office building because of exit facilities, it may be satisfactory for some facility which requires large space but few people.

When the architect or consultant is given a specific commission to find a building for a single specific use, his inspection must continue until he has found just the right building. When he is given a commission to recycle a specific building to a more profitable use, he must determine the best use and at the same time survey the building to determine whether this best use can be accomplished economically within the physical limitations of the structure.

This inspection of the adaptability of the building to any specific use leads inevitably to the next step, which is the investigation of the code requirements.

ZONING,

BUILDING CODE,

AND OSHA

REQUIREMENTS

4-1 ZONING

Before steps are taken toward acquiring any building for recycling or changing its use, the architect or the sponsor must determine whether the zoning ordinance allows such a use or conversely whether he can take advantage of one of the uses that is allowed.

Permitted Uses and Restrictions

Every zoning regulation contains a list of the uses that are permitted in a specific zone, and the principals involved in recycling are presumed to be familiar with them. They should also be familiar with floor-area ratios, height and bulk regulations, and other zoning requirements.

RESIDENTIAL ZONES AND DENSITY

Residential zones in larger communities permit multiple dwellings in all but their very highest classifications. The regulations also state that the number of housing units that can be built is determined by the size of the lot. This limitation changes with the zones. The limitation is further broken down by the kind of housing occupancy, i.e., apartments, efficiency apartments, housing for the elderly, and single rooms. For example, in an R5 zone (see Figs. 2-1 to 2-3) there must be 400 ft² of lot area per dwelling unit or 265 ft² per efficiency unit, etc. This means that on a 50- by 100-ft lot (5000 ft²) the architect can plan 12 apartments or 18 efficiency dwelling units. Knowing the allowable density in various zones is one of the prerequisites of the design.

RESTRICTED BUSINESS DISTRICTS

If the end use is to be an office building, several different use zones may be considered. For instance, a B4 zone allows a building to contain up to 18,750 ft² of office space. This means that a building on a 50- by 100-ft lot could have three or four floors of office space. Such a building can also have dwelling units instead of office space on the upper two or three floors or a shop or other retail establishment on the lower two or three floors.

In this zone a number of combinations of uses can be incorporated in the same building, depending on the requirements for space by various users. This zone, like some of the more restrictive commercial zones (C zones), gives the entrepreneur maximum flexibility.

Adverse Uses

The zoning map should also be examined to determine the locations of the zones which permit adverse uses. An adverse use is one that brings heavy truck traffic to the neighborhood, is noisy or dirty, or emits noxious fumes. Slum-clearance projects usually do not make good neighbors. Nearby superhighways or railroad tracks had not heretofore been thought desirable, but there has been a change in this thinking. Sometimes these rights-of-way can act as barriers to the infiltration of undesirable uses. Questioning of private-home owners whose property backs on a throughway has elicited the information that some owners prefer the noise of the throughway to the invasion of their back yards or neighborhood by adverse uses. They say they can live with the noise in order to enjoy the privacy.

Nonconforming Uses and Regulations

EXEMPTIONS

The structures ready for recycling are usually older ones and usually were built before the present zoning codes were adopted. Most of them do not conform to the new codes and are therefore now subject to more restrictive regulations. Most codes take cognizance of the fact that many of these structures are useful and well built and should not be condemned to the bulldozer. Therefore the codes specifically exempt such buildings from any present or future destruction (a permitted nonconforming use). The exemptions which allow the continued use of the building in its existing shape and bulk are:

Floor-area ratio

Front, side, or rear yards

Lot area per dwelling unit

Building height

Maximum gross floor area

Offstreet parking and loading areas

Allowable number of employees

Certain nonconforming uses and a provision that a nonconforming use cannot be invalidated by a change in title

All codes contain the provision that a building which has been occupied by a nonconforming use loses its exemption if this nonconforming use has been abandoned for more than 1 year. Codes also state that a nonconforming use can be changed to another nonconforming use if the new use "will have a lesser environmental impact upon the surrounding area than the old one."

ALTERATIONS AND ADDITIONS RELATING TO USE

Some codes do not allow any alterations except those required to correct building violations or safety hazards. Others allow structural repairs and replacements not to exceed[1] 20 percent of the current replacement value of a building. Alterations that exceed such values can be made only if the building is to conform to an allowed use. No additions of any kind can be made unless the building is to be changed to a conforming use.

The Application of Zoning to Recycling

The recycling entrepreneur will generally find that the local authority is receptive to his project and will go to some length to make it possible. All communities are sensitive to taxable property and will

---

[1]The 20 percent is exclusive of the cost of plans and foundations.

help to retain it or to make it more valuable in order to increase the assessed value.

Usually the purpose of any recycling project is to raise the property to a higher and therefore more profitable use. This is always permitted by zoning codes. It is nevertheless important for the entrepreneur to be familiar with all the nuances of the regulations.

4-2   BUILDING CODES

Restrictions on Altering the Use

Before any building can be recycled to a new use, there are at least two major provisions of any building code that must be considered. In general the zoning and building codes work hand in hand, but they differ where structural, mechanical, and fire-protection requirements are concerned. A zoning code will exempt a nonconforming building from certain of its current provisions (see exemptions in Sec. 4-1) if the new use is a permitted one or even if the new use, while not specifically permitted, has the same or less environmental impact than the old use. An example would be the recycling of a warehouse into an office building or multidwellings.

A building code contains no such exemptions. The change from a warehouse into an office building or a multiple dwelling would have to comply with current requirements for exit doors, stairways, fireproofing, sanitary facilities, occupancy standards, floor loading, heating, ventilation, plumbing, and possibly height and bulk. The reason should be obvious. *A zoning code protects the environment, property value, light, and air. A building code protects lives.*

Restrictions on the Cost of the Work

Even if the end product of the recycling is to be a continuation of the old use in a newly modernized building, the building code still provides for compliance with current code requirements under the following general provision:

> Existing buildings when altered or repaired . . . shall be made to conform to the full requirements of the code for new buildings:
>
>   1. If alterations or repairs are made within any period of 12 months, which cost in excess of 50% of the physical value of the building, or

2. If the cost of alterations or repairs . . . is between 25% and 50% of the physical value of the building, the building official shall determine to what degree the portion so altered or repaired shall be made to conform to the requirements for new buildings, or

3. If the cost of the alterations or repairs . . . is 25% or less . . . , the building official shall permit the restoration of the building to its *condition previous* to damage or deterioration with the *same kind of material* as those of which the building was constructed; *provided* that such construction does not endanger the general safety and public welfare. . . .

It can be seen from these requirements that the recycler is limited in the reconstruction of a building unless he goes to the expense of complying with current building codes. The only exceptions might be where the cost of conversion to a new use would be less than 25 percent of the value of the building. This might be when a warehouse is refurbished and changed to be used as a bulk filing center or an old loft or factory building is to be used again for manufacturing or product assembly.

However, there is nothing in these restrictions to frighten off a prospective entrepreneur. The change to a higher and more profitable use usually requires extensive alteration and reconstruction. Such extensive work should require very little additional planning or cost to assure compliance with the current code.

Building-Code Highlights

The architect or consultant is presumed to be as familiar with the basics of the building code as he is with the zoning code.

OCCUPANCY AND USE

The future occupancy of the building is a determining factor in the stringency of the code requirements. Some codes classify the occupancy under the term "use groups" or "classification of buildings by occupancy" or "occupancy classifications." A typical breakdown for such a classification would be:

High hazard. Buildings used for manufacturing or storage of potentially explosive or highly combustible material

Storage. Buildings used primarily for storing goods

Mercantile. Buildings used for display of goods for sale

Industrial. Manufacturing, assembling, and processing

Business.   Transacting business, rendering professional services with storage of a limited stock of goods for office use

Assembly.   Use by 75 persons or more for religious, recreational, educational, political, or similar uses

Educational.   Educational use of any kind

Institutional.   Use by persons with physical limitations

Residential.   Any use for human habitation

These classifications are further broken down into specific uses. What product is to be manufactured? What exactly will be the residential use? The determination of the precise use for the structure allows the architect to plan the recycling to comply with the structural, exit, ventilation, and other requirements for this type of occupancy. Codes contain exact details of required fire rating of walls and floors and of required exit requirements, etc.

BUILDING LIMITATIONS

The code limits the size of the building in three ways: (1) by type of occupancy, (2) by type of construction, and (3) by fire district.

All cities and most towns of any size have established boundary lines around their most heavily populated residential, business, and individual areas to define fire districts. The object of course is to prevent the spread of fire, and buildings within such districts are limited in size and in combustible construction.

Let us put all these limitations and restrictions into one example. A residential building with three or more dwelling units of semicombustible construction cannot be over 40 ft high or three stories high or contain more than 10,000 ft² of gross area in a district outside of the fire district and cannot be built at all in a fire district. An institutional building of the same construction is never allowed in any district.

OTHER IMPORTANT REQUIREMENTS

As part of the classification of the building, the codes allow various densities of occupancy. The exit requirements, the amount of ventilation, and the sanitary facilities are then designed to conform to these allowed densities. To some extent a building code resembles a nest of Chinese boxes because so many requirements must fit into other requirements. Nevertheless the architect must be familiar with them all.

4-3   OSHA REGULATIONS

Description

The Occupational Safety and Health Act, passed by Congress in 1970, is a set of regulations, enforceable by law, concerning the safety and health of the worker on construction or other occupational activity and the safety and health of all occupants of a structure. It adds one more dimension to the architect's design problems and one more tax on his ingenuity.

The OSHA regulations are in general more strict than many state laws, but many states already have adopted or will soon adopt this national code. In that case architects will not have to adapt the state or local law to this code. OSHA regulations are specially important in recycling because compliance may sometimes change a design concept which would be in accord with local or state code but not with OSHA regulations.

Important Provisions

JOB SAFETY

OSHA goes into great detail in the field of job safety. It is the builder's primary responsibility to maintain construction job safety, but the architect should be familiar with the provisions and should call the builder's attention to them. It is well also for others on the recycling team to be aware that there is an OSHA Act and that it is enforced by the federal government.

The Department of Labor Occupational Safety and Health Administration publishes Part 1910 of the Act, which applies specifically to the architect's and builder's concern.

GENERAL DESIGN CRITERIA

Stairways and means of egress   The regulations specify stair widths, heights, risers, treads, ramps, and facilities for both ingress and egress. Although the requirements agree with most local building codes, the designer should check them against each other.

Ventilation   OSHA's only concern with ventilation is in connection with the use of air contaminants or for certain industrial processes.

Sanitation   OSHA concerns itself to a large extent with buildings used for industrial or manufacturing purposes, but it also refers to buildings used for offices or other public use and to a small extent with residential construction.

In general, if the architect-engineer team designs to comply with a modern large-city or state code, it should have very little to worry about with regard to OSHA.

5

HOW A
DECISION IS
MADE

5-1 THE REQUIRED INPUT

Before the final decision can be made on a project, all the pertinent information in several fields of expertise must be summarized. The decision must indicate that this is the right structure in the right area and neighborhood to best serve the determined purpose. The decision must also contain conclusions on the total cost of the recycling; the appeal of the architecture, both exterior and interior; the needs of the market; the rate of return on the investment; and the financing. There are other decisions to be made, but they can be made later. The kind of information required will vary, depending on how a property is called to the attention of the recycling team. This may be a specific property to begin with, or the recycling team may be given a commission to find a property that is to be converted for a specific use. The architect, the real estate consultant, or the developer aware of a market need will search for a property to meet this need, or they may just search for any property that seems a fit subject for recycling.

31

5-2 HOW TO DETERMINE A PROFITABLE USE FOR A SPECIFIC STRUCTURE

Sometimes an owner is dissatisfied with the rate of return on his property because it is partly vacant or underutilized and possibly in a state of disrepair. He wants the building to be recycled to a use which will entail modernization and repair and at the same time bring him a higher rate of return.

The principal may be a lessee who no longer has any use for the structure but whose lease still has many years to run. His objective is the same as if he were the owner.

The principal may be one who has purchased an abandoned property such as a school, a hospital, a warehouse, a railroad station, a loft, or manufacturing building and who now wishes to recycle the property to a profitable use.

The property may be an almost new apartment house or office building or condominium whose owner has found that he has built in the wrong place at the wrong time. He wishes to change the structure to a more profitable use.

In any of the above examples the architect or another member of the recycling team may have initiated the project by approaching the owner with an offer to bring the property to more profitable long-term use.

The Information Required

When the property is a specific one, some of the preliminary steps can be eliminated.

THE REAL ESTATE CONSULTANT

When he has a specific property in mind, the real estate consultant must decide on the best and most profitable use for it. He has a choice of the many uses set forth in Chap. 1, as well as others. He must be aware of the population and business trends in the general area and in the specific neighborhood. He should be aware of the special needs of the community such as office space, living space, factory space, etc., or unexpressed needs such as studios, art galleries, showrooms, health-care centers, and so forth. He must be guided by the size, shape, and appearance of the structure and informed about tax and assessment rates, management costs, the sources of financing, and any possible conflict with present or future redevelopment authority.

THE BROKER

The real estate consultant and the rental broker may be one and the same; if not, the consultant should have access to information gathered by a broker. Many brokers manage property and have figures on rental rates, management costs, and occupancy percentages. Brokers who do not manage property and do not have specific management costs have means of obtaining them, and they have information on rental and occupancy rates of business and residential property as well as the locations where rental or sales activity is taking place.

THE ARCHITECT-ENGINEER TEAM

This team must make a feasibility study of the building to determine whether the use that has been determined can be achieved architecturally, structurally, mechanically, and within a budget. The determined use comes as a result of a meeting of the minds of the owner, the consultant, the broker, and sometimes the architect and a builder.

In numerous instances the architect has been the prime mover. The feasibility study must consist of certain essential elements:

Study of the zoning code to ascertain whether the determined use is allowed or can be obtained by an appeal

Study of the building code to determine whether its requirements for the proposed type of occupancy create any excessively expensive structural or mechanical changes

Sketches and calculations to determine the maximum area for which rent can be charged, e.g., the number of salable rooms in condominiums or rentable rooms in rental apartments, or square feet of office, storage, filing, or computer area or the number of beds in a nursing home

The preliminary line drawings and outline specifications indicating the work to be done and the estimated cost of doing it

THE CONSTRUCTION CONTRACTOR

The builder may be a member of the recycling team, or he may be employed under a contractual arrangement. Even if it has been decided to let the contract by competitive bidding, a knowledgeable and experienced alteration contractor should be called in under a fee arrangement to look over the architect-engineer's shoulder as the design proceeds. This contractor can consult structural and mechanical subcontractors for advice and for "ball park" estimates.

5-3 HOW TO LOCATE A PROPERTY FOR A SPECIFIC USE

This type of recycling project occurs when a property must be found to serve a specific need. A factory, assembly plant, or office occupant may require expansion space, or any user or proposed user may require space to carry on a specific activity.

Locating the Building

The recycler must now go through the additional steps of area and neighborhood surveys. He must also make a survey of buildings in the appropriate locations in order to find the right building for the specific purpose.

THE REAL ESTATE CONSULTANT (AND BROKER)

When there is a specific use in mind, the consultant has to find the appropriate area and neighborhood in which such a use will fit. If the object of the recycling is to add space in another location for expansion of a present use, he must examine the means of communication and transportation between the several locations of the business. But whether it is expansion or complete relocation, he should follow the steps outlined in Chap. 2 in order to make sure that the location is viable.

The broker can be of great help here because he will know the buildings that have been sold or are for sale and the going prices. He should also be aware of movements and activity in the various locations under consideration.

THE ARCHITECT-ENGINEER

The first act of the architect must be to examine the building or buildings that have been tentatively chosen to make sure that the size, shape, and architecture (or external appearance) will be pleasing to the client who has commissioned the project. This could be called the *aesthetic evaluation*. Next the architect must check the interior both structurally and mechanically and determine the optimum amount of space available for specific use. The architect has a duty in this case, as in any case of building or recycling, to study the zoning and building codes.

THE CONSTRUCTION CONTRACTOR

His duties have been set forth in Sec. 5-2.

5-4   RECYCLING PROJECTS

An architect, a developer-builder, or any investor may be interested in a recycling project on a speculative basis. He will be willing to find a property that can be purchased at a reasonable price and recycled for any market need. The primary motivation in this case is the profit.

Such a project should have the benefit of all the information available from market surveys, area and neighborhood surveys, rental and property-cost information, and other sources. These can be the same as for any specific recycling project, but the scope should be greater in order to cover all possible kinds of final uses. For instance, the zoning code for any considered area should allow such diverse uses as multifamily dwellings, office-building use, showrooms, light service uses, etc., and of course there are many areas that allow such uses. The same is true for the building code. A structure may be found which can be recycled at moderate cost for some uses but which would be too costly to change to a multiple dwelling or for institutional use.

The architect has to produce alternate designs for use of the space for various purposes, and the construction contractor has to price each design. In a case of this kind at least some participants may be asked to contribute their time as a speculative venture.

The financial reward in a successful venture of this kind is much greater because the recycling team (or part of it) is the owner of the property. It therefore obtains not only its fees but the speculative profit as well.

5-5   FINANCIAL CONSIDERATIONS

With the exception of publicly financed recyclings and historical preservations subsidized or financed by the government, recycling projects should not be considered unless it can be demonstrated that they will be profitable. Outside financing will be required even for a specific building whose owner is the principal of the team or when a property is to found, purchased, and recycled for a specific use by a specific enterprise. Financial institutions or groups with money to lend will not consider lending any money unless they are assured that they will get it back with interest or as a participation or other form of profit. It should be unnecessary to mention this, but many would-be borrowers seem to lose sight of this fact of life.

At the point of decision it is therefore necessary to gather together the financial facts to summarize and reinforce all the other information that has been gathered.

Investigation of the Total Estimated Cost of the Project

The first step in such a financial statement (which in effect summarizes the feasibility of a recycling project) is a determination of the estimated total cost to completion. This must be arrived at by a careful and informed study made by experts in the field. It should convince the lender as well as reveal the facts to the recycler and thereby prevent a possible serious loss on his part.

The items of cost that enter into a summary of total cost are:

Cost of the property including all professional fees, all take-over costs (taxes, fuel, utilities, etc.)

Cost of preparing surveys (real estate consultant, broker, architect, engineer)

Cost of preparing initial (or outline) plans and specifications and fee to contractor for preliminary estimates of cost

Estimated construction cost of recycling including total fee of the architect-engineer, cost of permits, legal, administration, project manager (if any)

Cost of marketing the project (advertising, signs, brokerage fees)

Any rental costs, including estimated costs of partitions, etc., for tenants

Investigation of the Possible Rental Scale (The Income)

What is the projected rental income? This amount must be investigated and estimated no matter what kind of recycling is to be done. Even an enterprise that specifically authorizes the search for a property to purchase and recycle for its own use has to charge itself rent. The real estate consultant and the broker must be able to make available the following information.

Location of buildings that are being used for the same purpose and description of their neighborhoods

Descriptions of these buildings in detail, e.g., height, floor area, rentable square feet or number of apartments; description of services, general appearance, type of tenants, and a photograph

Rent roll per square foot or per different type of apartment or per room, etc.; percentage of occupancy; renting or sales activity

Prices asked and paid for condominium apartments of similar size and in similar locations

Forecast of escalation for taxes and operating costs

The projected rental for a recycled project to be occupied by the owner must be realistic if the project is to be financed by outside sources and should also take IRS and other taxing agencies into account. It is suggested that a tax expert be consulted from the very beginning. There are many cases where government subsidies are available. Some cities forgive part of the real estate tax, and in recycling the IRS can be lenient with tax shelters.

Investigation of the Operating Cost

Here again the numbers should come from the real estate consultant and the broker. They are the people who have access to such records. The typical headings under which general costs of operation go are shown in Table 5-1. If the Table 5-1 seems too detailed, the following shorter list of expenses will serve most purposes:

Cleaning

Electrical

Heating and air conditioning

Plumbing

Elevators

General

Administrative including legal

Accounting etc.

Leasing

Alterations and painting

TABLE 5-1 CLASSIFICATION OF GENERAL COSTS OF OPERATION

Category	Breakdown
Compensation	Janitors, porters, handymen, painters, resident manager, guards, gardeners, matrons, wall washers, carpenters (group insurance, pensions, FOAB, any other benefits)
Operating	Building cleaning (by outside contractor), cleaning supplies, window cleaning, heating and air conditioning, including fuel cost, venetian blinds, water and sewer costs, washroom supplies, rubbish, exterminating, building office supplies, uniforms, telephone, travel expenses, lighting cost including lamps and fixture repair, professional expense, leasing expense
Maintenance and repairs	All supplies for electrical, plumbing, painting, heating, ventilating, and air conditioning (HVAC), cost of repairs and maintenance by outside contractors such as roofing, plumbing, electrical, HVAC, grounds, elevators
Insurance	Fire, liability, boiler, automobile liability, property damage, workmen's compensation
Taxes and assessments	
Administrative expenses	

Repairs

Insurance

Real estate taxes

Grounds and landscaping

5-6 THE INCOME AND EXPENSE STATEMENT

This statement should summarize the financial facts of the project. It should show the final total estimated cost and the estimated operating cost, including taxes and the estimated income. There should be solid background information for all these figures.

This is the statement the lender will study carefully. It must show that after all operating, maintenance, insurance, taxes, and other costs are paid there will be more than enough money to pay the debt service, which is the interest and amortization on the required mortgage. From such a summary statement the entrepreneur should assure himself that he will earn a reasonable rate of return on his own equity money (which should include cost for time as well as actual money). (A sample income and expense statement is shown in Table 6-1.)

The statement must of course show the amount of money that is required and the amount of the debt service as well as the equity money to be invested by the owner.

5-7   THE DECISION

The final decision to proceed with a recycling project is really a financial one. This book is not about historical preservations as such, although the project may very well be one, like the Ironfronts in Richmond (Chap. 19). It is a book about profitable recycling. The owner(s) must take into consideration the long-range profitability of the project by looking at the trend of the area, the neighborhood, and the purpose of the building. Architectural preservation is important, but it cannot be the first consideration.

FINANCING

THE PROJECT

6-1   ASSEMBLING THE NECESSARY INFORMATION

When all the groundwork has been completed and it has been decided what to recycle, where it will be, what its final use will be, and how profitable it will be, the entrepreneur is ready for the final application to a lender for funds.

Construction money and a permanent mortgage are not as easy to obtain for recycling as funds for a new project in an established or growing area or neighborhood. Nevertheless, money is available for recycling if it can be proved to the satisfaction of the lender that the project is sound and will be profitable for the foreseeable future. It should again be emphasized that no money either for construction or a permanent loan will be forthcoming unless the lender is reasonably assured that he will get his money back with interest.

Before approaching anyone for funds, the entrepreneur must assemble certain data.

The Results of an Area and Neighborhood Survey

If the lender is an institution, it will be aware of the general trend of the area and the community. However, the applicant should pinpoint the structure he is interested in and be able to state why the location is good for that particular use. If the lender is an individual or a fund, it may not have all the general data, which the applicant must be prepared to furnish. Any prospective recycler should avoid so called *redlined districts*. Although red lining is frowned upon by government, it is still a factor in mortgage lending. In any case the recycler is advised to avoid such areas. Rehabilitation in such areas must be subsidized.

The Marketing Conclusions

Such a statement should include the results of a rental survey of a comparable building for comparable use, a survey of vacant space, and a statement of what is being done and will be done to promote the rental (or sale) of the space.

The Architectural and Structural Considerations

It is true that a lender will not be persuaded to finance a project because of its architectural treatment, but he will certainly be favorably impressed by a recycling project that preserves good architecture and is shown to be structurally sound before work begins.

The applicant should be able to produce the results of a survey of the structural integrity of the project and enough plans and specifications to show the lender exactly what he proposes to do to reinforce the structure if necessary and to bring the structure up to the modern mechanical and electrical standards required by present-day tenants.

6-2 PREPARING THE LOAN APPLICATION

The purpose of the application is to convince the prospective lender that this is a sound project which will produce sufficient cash flow to pay back the borrowed money plus a satisfactory rate of interest on the investment. The statement must therefore show all the facts (see Table 6-1).

The last portion of the application should show the amount of the debt service compared with the total cash flow. Such an amount cannot

TABLE 6-1 SUGGESTED TABULATION OF NECESSARY INFORMATION

Location of project
  Land size and building size
  Complete description of property (exhibits to include street scenes, applicable zoning code, photographs of existing building and a rendering of finished building, report on age and physical conditions of the existing structure, outline plans and specifications of work to be done)
Cost of original property
  Land cost per square foot
  Cost of existing building per square foot of gross area
  Acquisition cost (including finder's fee; brokerage, legal, and closing costs; administrative expense)
Estimated cost of recycling ready for occupancy
  Estimated construction cost including tenant work based on contractors' estimates
  Architects', engineers', and other technical fees
  Cost of permits and other filing fees
  Legal and administrative costs
  Cost accounting, recordkeeping, etc.
  Insurance during construction
  Taxes during construction
  Estimated interest on construction loan
  Fees or commissions for obtaining mortgage
Total cost of project ready for occupancy
Amount of mortgage money required
Owner's equity
Estimated income
  Schedule A: breakdown of estimated rents*
    Basement   _____ft^2 at \$_____
    Ground or first floor:
      Streetfront stores   _____ft^2 at \$_____
      Rear areas   _____ft^2 at \$_____
    Second floor   _____ft^2 at \$_____
    Third floor   _____ft^2 at \$_____
    or
    First floor
      1½–2 rooms at _____
      2–2½ rooms at _____
      2–3 rooms at _____
    Second floor†
    Third floor†
Estimated operating expense‡
  Janitorial services (payroll or contract), including office space, corridors, toilet rooms, window washing
  Janitorial supplies
  Handyman, boiler attendant, etc., including all mechanical service personnel on payroll
  Plumbing, contract work
  Electrical, contract work, including lamping
  General maintenance supplies

TABLE 6-1   SUGGESTED TABULATION OF NECESSARY INFORMATION

Elevator maintenance, contract
Exterminating, contract
Refuse (if not included in taxes)
Painting and decorating (lease terms)
HVAC including fuel cost and maintenance contract
Utilities (gas, electricity, water, sewer)
Insurance (fire and extended coverage, liability, compensation, etc.)
Taxes (real estate, improvement, etc.)
Management cost (whether by owner or management agent)
Miscellaneous
Income less expense
Interest and amortization on requested financing
Remaining cash flow for return on equity
Percentage return on equity

---

*Can be on a separate sheet.

†Give same information as for first floor.

‡Can be calculated on a per square foot basis.

be shown unless the owner has a very good idea that the lender to whom he applies is willing to advance funds at the rate of interest, amortization, and for the term of years shown.

6-3   SOURCES OF FINANCING

In order to assure himself of funds when he requires them, i.e., at the start of construction, the entrepreneur must start looking for financing as soon as he has gathered sufficient information, as shown in Sec. 6-2. The location of the project has a great deal to do with the kind of lending institution he approaches. He should apply for both a construction loan and a permanent loan. If permanent financing is arranged, the construction financing is comparatively simple to obtain and often the permanent lender will also be the construction lender.

Insurance Companies

In a city or a large town when a loan is over $1 million it is recommended that a life insurance company be approached. These institutions are conservative lenders, but in the past few years they have become receptive to recycling loans. Many of these companies have salaried agents or loan correspondents in the larger cities.

Foundation and Other Funds

For large loans in large communities there are also pension funds, trust funds, and foundations. This kind of institution does not have local offices and usually works through a local mortgage broker, who must of course be paid a commission for finding the loan.

Savings Banks

Savings banks are an excellent source of financing and are very receptive to local enterprise. The large big-city savings banks are usually willing to consider loans almost statewide, and the smaller-town banks will certainly consider countywide loans.

Building and Loan Societies

Building and loan institutions favor residential loans and will also consider condominiums, blanket loans, and subsequent individual loans to the purchasers of the units.

Endowment Funds

College and university endowment funds are sometimes available for large loans in large cities, but again such funds are usually available only through a mortgage broker. Whenever direct contact is not possible, a simple letter of inquiry to a foundation or college endowment or pension fund which gives some of the basic facts may bring surprising results.

Commercial Banks

Commercial banks seldom make permanent loans, but they are very receptive to construction loans once a permanent commitment has been obtained.

Real Estate Investment Trusts (REIT)

Some REITs are still in existence, and their business is to finance the construction and ownership of real estate. They have become very careful about the loans they consider because so many of them have been hurt in recent years by bad loans.

Private Financing

When the required funds do not run over six figures, it may be possible to obtain private financing from an individual or a group of individuals who may form a consortium to take over the permanent loan. Such a group, however, is likely to ask for a higher than customary rate of return and is more likely to be interested in providing equity or seed money for a participation in the ownership. This kind of venture capital is always available if one knows where to find it. Mortgage brokers as well as local banks are most likely to know about it. Real estate bulletins or publications are likely to mention possible sources of such financing.

FHA Guarantees

For multifamily residential property, whether rental or condominium, it is possible to obtain FHA approval for a loan which then, because of the government guarantee, makes it much simpler to obtain an institutional loan. To obtain such a guarantee, however, the owner must allow several months of lead time for the required paper work and for gathering the information required by FHA regulations.

Now that the recycling of buildings has received national prominence, it should not be too difficult to obtain both construction and financing for a well-thought-out and soundly organized recycling project.

7

THE ARCHITECT'S
CONTRACT

7-1 THE PARTIES TO THE CONTRACT

In the usual construction project the owner engages an architect-engineer to produce a set of plans and specifications in accordance with the owner's requirements. In recycling a building for a specific purpose the architect may also be working under a specific set of instructions. In many recyclings, however, it is the architect who is the leadman, the one with the imagination to see how an abandoned warehouse can become an office building or an abandoned hospital a condominium. In these cases the architect has become a party at interest. He is financially involved both in his professional capacity and as a member of a profit-oriented group. Even when the architect is the sole promoter, he must still act in a dual capacity because the mortgage lender and the construction lender will require that he clearly define his separate interests.

He must therefore perform his work under a clearly defined contract whether he is working for an owner or for himself.

7-2   PROVISIONS COMMON TO ALL CONTRACTS

A number of basic provisions are common to all contracts between the owner and the architect. While the actual wording of a contract states that the parties to it must come to an agreement before work starts, the following is what it really means.

Owner's Obligations

The owner must furnish a program of his requirements. What kind of end use does he want? What kind of tenants does he want? What quality of construction does he want? What is the timetable? The owner, whoever he may be, makes these decisions based to a large extent on financial considerations.

Architect's Obligations

The architect must review the program for its practicality and its cost. He must advise the owner how he can best attain his objective. He is responsible for the design, both interior and exterior. He must advise the owner about quality and what it may cost. There must be a meeting of minds between owner and architect before any drawings or specifications are started. Some but not all of the architect's possible obligations are listed below.

1. He is expected to visit the job often enough to assure himself that the work is being done in strict accordance with the plans and specifications. When large projects are being constructed, contracts often call for a full-time representative of the architect-engineer to be on the job.

2. He should act as the owner's representative in issuing instructions to the contractor. Such instructions may involve changes in design or materials, and it is the architect-engineer's duty to see that such changes in work are performed properly and at a fair cost.

3. He should be on the job often enough to be able to approve progress payments to the contractor. This should be done by means of a form signed by the architect and known as a *certificate of payment.*

4. He must serve as the judge in disputes between the owner and the contractor, and his interpretation of the plans and specifications is considered final.

5. He has the authority and the duty to reject work or material which he feels does not meet the specifications. He must also issue change orders subject to the owner's approval and must check and approve shop drawings.

6. He must keep close account of progress and should call the contractor's and owner's attention to the possible failure to comply with the schedule of completion. He can also suggest ways in which such lack of progress can be overcome, sometimes by substitution of more available labor or material than that specified.

Progress of Design

Every contract should provide for certain design steps to be taken, each of which is to be approved by the owner before the next step is begun. This is a good thing to do no matter who the owner is. It gives all parties a chance to sit back and reflect before spending more time and money on plan development. There are usually schematic line drawings, then design-development drawings, and finally working drawings and contract documents.

Other Basic Provisions

The usual contract also contains provisions for the cancellation of the contract, for arbitration, for payments, for maintenance of records, etc.

7-3   TYPES OF CONTRACTS

The difference in contract provision has to do mostly with how the architect's compensation is calculated. There are four basic types.

Percentage of Construction Cost

This contract is probably more widely used than any other. It assures the owner that the fee will be within certain fixed limits, and it assures the architect of a fair fee. It should exactly define the architect-engineer's duties and what the cost of the work consists of. Such exact definitions, if agreed upon beforehand, can eliminate many future disputes and claims and counterclaims for extras or delays. The amount of the percentage depends on several factors. The first is the complexity of the project. A stipulated-sum construction contract on a new construction project would obviously be the simplest to administer. In recycling, however, while the construction contract may be for a stipulated sum, the administration of the contract is far from simple. It requires constant attention on the part of the architect to see that the wrong thing is not demolished and that proper connections and alterations are made to existing installations. If the contract is not for a stipulated sum but is based on a guaranteed maximum price or, worse, is based on a cost plus fee, the architect's administration becomes quite difficult and the amount of the percentage should reflect this fact. These contracts also provide for additional compensation for work beyond original scope and for clearly defined expenses.

Fixed Fee

A surprising number of fixed-fee contracts occur in recycling projects. All such contracts call for additional compensation for work beyond the original agreed-upon scope. The original scope must therefore be very clearly defined and agreed to by both parties. How the amount of extra compensation is arrived at must also be clearly defined.

Fee Plus Expenses

This contract is the same as a cost plus fixed fee construction contract. The architect charges a professional fee for his expertise. Then he bills for all his labor costs, including his own, to all of which is added a multiple for overhead. He also bills for expenses and consulting work by others. There does not really seem to be any compelling reason for this type of contract. There is no incentive other than the architect's professionalism to perform quickly or accurately. The owner cannot accurately budget the cost, and a prospective lender could be very unhappy about this undefined expense. If such a contract must be made, every single item of cost that is to be allowed must be defined. This includes the actual payroll plus its multiple (with a provision that no increases in pay will be honored without prior consent), clearly defined expenses, principal's rate of pay, etc.; the contract must also state that the owner has the right to audit the architect's books at any time.

Multiple of Direct Personnel Expense

This type of agreement is very often used when an owner is not certain when and how he will perform a recycling. He may be considering several properties, and he may want an architect-engineer's professional advice on how best to recycle such properties for the use he requires. This may involve sketches and enough specifications so that he can obtain an idea of what the recycling may cost. In such cases the simplest form of architect's contract is one by which the owner pays to the architect a sum consisting of the architect's time multiplied by an agreed hourly rate, plus the architect's employees' time multiplied by an hourly rate, plus any consultant's bills times a multiple. He also pays for specified expenses. An owner can set a total sum for such services which cannot be exceeded unless an additional sum is authorized.

It is suggested that this form of contract be used only until the character and the extent of the project is decided. At that time it would be best for all concerned to enter into a fixed-fee or percentage-of-construction-cost contract.

8

DETAILED STUDY

OF THE

STRUCTURE

Before the architect and the engineer start the final design, they make a thorough structural, mechanical, and architectural survey of the present structure. There will also be a survey of the available space and its layout. In many cases the plans and specifications of the structure will no longer be available, so that everything must be measured and the existing structural and mechanical installation investigated. These measurements and other findings provide the basic facts for the final plans and specifications. The importance of the space survey can be illustrated by a recent example. An old apartment house was recycled as a condominium. The architect created several duplex units by breaking through floors and providing attractive spiral stairways. These units proved so popular that they were sold before they were completed. Several first-floor apartments were located just over some basement space, which was above grade. These single-floor units could have been converted into duplexes with the lower floor located in the basement, and they would have sold; but because a thorough survey was not made, they were sold as one-floor units and the basement space is being used only for social or storage purposes, providing little or no income.

The initial survey of the structure must be made with the building code regulations and the final use of the building always in mind. Experience shows what should be examined, as follows.

8-1   THE FOUNDATIONS AND THE BASEMENT

Any signs of cracking or spalling in a masonry wall or any signs of settling of basement floors or an uneven level in the upper floors will immediately alert the architect to the possibility of a foundation problem. Other signs of settling can be detected from window sills or cornices. Instead of relying on the eye it is recommended that a surveying instrument be used for levels and for ascertaining the plumb of the walls and the structure in general. Usually any structure with foundation or settlement problem should be dropped from consideration, but there may be special instances in which the price of the building and its area and height, etc., may just be suitable for the final use. If this is true and the settling is not too severe, a test boring or two may reveal the cause of the problem. The ultimate load to be placed on the structure can be the deciding factor.

Determining the available space in the basement is very important. It may be possible to use it as a work space, for which rent can be collected, and there should be storage space for tenants. There should be space for a chiller unit, fans, and a heating plant and headroom for ductwork. The building code should be examined for fireproofing requirements.

8-2   STRUCTURAL CHARACTERISTICS

As the inspection now goes beyond such easily determinable factors as column spacing and floor heights, the architect must analyze the structural strength of the supporting structure. If original plans are not available, some of the ceiling, walls, and column coverings must be removed to reveal the underlying structure. Timber construction, especially in the lower floors or under the roof, must be checked for insect infestation or rot. Iron or steel must be checked for corrosion, loose bolting, proper bearings, etc.

Generally most older buildings have more than sufficient structural strength in their exterior bearing walls and in their interior structure to satisfy present-day codes for floor loading and other structural requirements. Some uses, however, require heavier loading than was contemplated in the original design. In such cases supportive structures must be designed. This can also occur when existing floor heights lend themselves to division into two floors. This occurs in one of the case studies (Chap. 20).

Interior bearing walls should be examined for cracks, loose mortar joints, proper bearing on foundations, and proper support of structural members.

8-3   THE FLOOR SYSTEM

The floor system in older buildings is usually strong enough to satisfy present codes. If not, a supportive structure or individual supportive members may be necessary. The architect should also keep in mind the spacing of the existing girders or other support members so that he can design his interior partitioning to allow filing, storage, heavy machinery, etc., over such existing members or reinforced members. The floor system should also be examined to determine whether shaft space for additional stairways, vertical plumbing, heating, electrical, air conditioning, or other utilities can be cut through it and framed without excessive expense. How about an elevator? The future interior design and use and the existing or reinforced structural design must complement each other. It is very expensive to come back later, as every architect knows.

8-4   THE EXTERIOR WALLS

The exterior walls should be examined for many reasons. First, their physical condition must be determined. Such things as a combination of horizontal and vertical cracks, watertightness, condition of flashings, and loose mortar joints should be looked for. An important point in the examination of the exterior walls is to determine whether they can be safely pierced for additional windows, for ventilation, or air conditioning.

The condition of the fenestration (its flashing, its caulking, its adaptability for new use, and its general condition) must be ascertained. New fenestration is expensive to purchase and install. It may have to be especially made to fit the existing openings, or the existing openings may have to be adapted to available sizes.

8-5 MECHANICAL AND ELECTRICAL EQUIPMENT

The candidate for recycling does not usually contain modern or even usable mechanical and electrical piping, wiring, or equipment. If the building is not too old, it may have some usable boilers, ducts, motors, fans, etc. The architect must bear in mind, however, that recycling a building involves compliance with the present code.

Heating

Start with the heating plant. Is it of sufficient capacity to heat the structure adequately after renovation? Possibly the building is to be used for a manufacturing process that requires additional heating (or cooling). How is the heat distributed now? The boiler and burner (or stoker, etc.) and the piping should be examined by an expert. It is possible that a great deal of it can be salvaged. Screw piping looks very good until it has to be relocated and recut, at which point it may disintegrate. Several pieces of piping should be backed off from their fittings to see whether this is likely to happen.

Ventilation

This depends on how the building will be used. Certain manufacturing processes must have forced ventilation, and office buildings or other commercially used buildings must be ventilated in accordance with their population; interior sanitary facilities must always be ventilated. Of course, any architect or engineer is familiar with these requirements. The purpose of this section is simply to remind him that he must provide shaft space for these requirements and space for the necessary fan equipment. Even if the existing structure contains some ductwork, this should be tested carefully for obstructions, deterioration, air leakage, or sharp bends. The adequacy of its size must also be verified.

Air Conditioning

The air conditioning of a recycled building is almost wholly a question of economic feasibility. The quality and the cost must be balanced against the expected occupancy and rental income. In inspecting the existing structure care must be taken to ensure sufficient headroom for ducts, sufficient shaft space for feeder ducts, and sufficient space for the chiller unit and the fans. If window units or fan-coil units are contemplated, can the exterior wall be pierced without defacing or seriously damaging the structure?

Plumbing

Plumbing lines, especially in old buildings which used galvanized-iron water lines, should be carefully checked. In areas where soft water is supplied, they are subject to serious deterioration. Even if the lines look good from the outside, some of them should be backed off from their fittings and examined closely for interior deterioration. The locations of the waste and vent lines should be spotted to determine whether the shafts at least can be reused for new toilet rooms and other plumbing facilities. The location and character of the water and sewer connections to street lines must be determined. Depending on the future use of the building, both these lines may have to be enlarged. New codes contain definite provisions for the size of these lines and for traps, cleanouts, etc. If sprinklers are to be used, there must be a separate line for them. There are also rules for pumps, roof tanks, pressure testing, etc. Any plumbing lines that are to be reused must comply with all of these rules.

Electrical

In recycling a building which predates the adoption of the present electrical code the architect and engineer should be prepared to renew the electrical system almost in its entirety. Present codes call for panel boards, junction boxes, protection of electrical feeders, etc., that were nonexistent not many years ago. The architect and engineer must also determine whether a new transformer vault and new feeder lines are necessary. Shaft space for vertical feeders must also be available. The local utility should be asked for its requirements, which in some cases can be quite expensive and difficult to accomplish.

8-6 ROOF AND WATERPROOFING

The roof, the parapets, and the cornices are parts of an existing structure that are subject to severe deterioration. Many older buildings have projecting metal cornices which are almost certain to be corroded and even unsafe. It is strongly advised that any projecting metal cornice be very carefully examined if the architect plans to continue its use. If the cornice is of terra cotta or stone, the anchorage should be carefully examined for corrosion. Parapets and flashings should also be carefully examined for cracks and loose mortar. A careful examination of the top-floor ceiling may reveal water leakage through the roof, the flashings, the cornices, or the parapets.

Most older buildings that are ready for recycling require a complete new roof. In any case, if the roof is to be insulated (as it should be), a new roof, flashings, etc., will be necessary.

8-7 STAIRWAYS AND EXITS

When examining the structure for stair and exit facilities, the architect should constantly consult the building code. If these facilities are not adequate in size, number, or location, where can new ones be placed? Is the structural system adaptable to framing for large openings? It goes without saying that the exit facilities and the future floor plans are complementary.

Exit facilities to grade must have unobstructed access to streets. Many old buildings are built right up to the lot line. Exit doors leading to such areas are not acceptable.

Even if stairways are sufficient in size and location, they may not meet code requirements for fire safety.

8-8 ADAPTABILITY OF STRUCTURE FOR RECYCLING

This study is really the factor deciding what can be done with the building, whether it can be done economically, and whether it will have rental or sales appeal.

While the building may be structurally sound and able to meet the size and height required for its final purpose, within reasonable limits, its interior arrangement must be such that it can be adapted to its final use without major structural changes.

To repeat some of the inspection items mentioned in previous sections of this chapter:

Is the structure of the floor suitable for the cutting of shafts, stairways, etc.?

Is the column spacing adaptable to the partitioning off of workable areas?

Is the fenestration spacing adaptable to partitioning off workable areas? Many older buildings which have their windows separated by masonry mullions have been found to be quite adaptable to modern office-size modules.

Does floor-to-floor height pose any problem? Many older buildings have high ceilings, especially on the street floor. A mezzanine or even a full second floor should be carefully considered for additional usable or rentable space. All floor heights must be sufficient for a hung ceiling in order to provide space for lighting and air conditioning.

Is it possible to install an elevator?

Is there sufficient space for all necessary mechanical and electrical equipment?

Is there storage space for tenants, including shops?

8-9 SALVAGE

Many items that must be removed from an old structure have definite salvage value. They may be more trouble to remove intact, but this cost should be balanced against their salvage value. Some examples follow:

Steel structural members

Sheet metal and piping (especially lead or brass)

Hardware

Hard-wood flooring, moldings, paneling

Old timbers

Fireplaces

Tiling

Old brick or stone

In a nearby town a large yard owned by a wrecking company displays and sells the most unlikely objects and materials from old houses and at most unlikely prices, but it appears to be a prosperous venture.

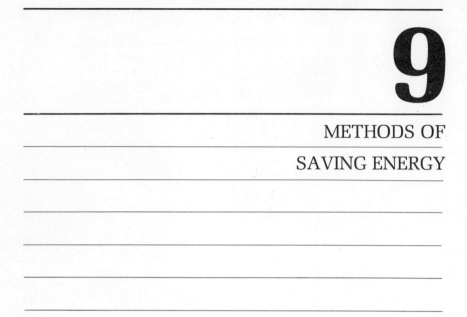

9

METHODS OF

SAVING ENERGY

9-1 GENERAL CONSIDERATIONS

The energy crisis presents great opportunities for the recycling entre-preneur to make a contribution to the national effort and save many dollars in operating costs.

Cost

Many energy-saving installations can be made at minimal cost and should be done in any recycling. Other measures for energy savings add considerably to the initial cost of construction but pay for them-selves in savings over a period of years. Such savings will become larger as the cost of energy inevitably increases.

The Economics

The final use of the structure and the ultimate ownership can be the determining factor in how much work is done. If the recyclers are to be the owners, it is recommended that as much as possible be done even at some extra expense and even if the payoff of the additional investment takes a few years. If the recycling is being accomplished for a client-owner or another ultimate user, the architect should make every effort to convince him that the extra expense is more than justified.

The Engineering

Careful engineering calculations must be made to ensure that each device or duct or piping method will eventually pay for itself (3 to 5 years) and will not be just a gadget. The recycler must be fully aware of the fact that many devices that are supposed to save energy do so only in special cases and under certain conditions. The local climate, the specific area conditions (wind, sun, exposure), and the siting of the building are all important.

9-2   ENERGY-SAVING CODE REQUIREMENTS

Why They Are Necessary

Many commercial structures, whether new or recycled, consider energy wastage as part of the overhead cost. This is not done deliberately but because energy conservation has not yet become a serious consideration. According to owners and redevelopers, the initial cost of the structure is the most important item in the financial statement, and most lenders are not yet sympathetic toward the additional expense necessary to provide the savings in operating costs. Even such public buildings as schools, town halls, etc., are reluctant to add to the initial cost, in spite of the fact that the taxpayer will have to pay higher operating expenses for many years to come. Only recently has the financial community become aware of this situation, and few local governments have as yet alerted the taxpayer.

Governmental Regulation

The answer to the lack of voluntary effort is government regulation through building codes, through FHA, HUD, or other federal or local government agencies which have the power to withhold loans or deny building permits. Within the past few years the government has begun to regulate the use of energy for public buildings and various agency-financed buildings. The General Services Administration has issued guidelines for public buildings. In 1973 the Department of Housing and Urban Development (HUD) issued a set of Minimum Property

Standards. The National Conference of States on Building Codes and Standards has asked the National Bureau of Standards to prepare guidelines for the ultimate inclusion in building codes.

Methods of Enforcing Conservation

There are several ways in which the use of energy in a structure can be controlled by code. One of the simpler ones is by limiting the amount of heat loss through all surfaces of the structure exposed to the weather. This can be done by specifying the maximum coefficient of heat transmission U that will be allowed through each surface before a building permit is issued. The architect can accomplish this in several ways without too much interference with his design. Another possible method of control by code is to limit the heat loss (or gain) based on the area or cubage of the structure.

The entrepreneur contemplating recycling should remember that while building codes are not generally retroactive, they can become so if the general welfare so dictates. A local law enacted by the City of New York to promote fire safety in existing high-rise buildings by the installation of sprinklers or other equally expensive alterations is a case in point.

9-3 DESIGN CRITERIA FOR ENERGY CONSERVATION

It is not the purpose of this book or this chapter to burden the prospective recycler with complicated or excessive engineering data. Instead there will be lists of broad design parameters and of smaller design changes and maintenance items which can be performed without excessive cost. These, of course, apply to large as well as small buildings. The owner or recycler is strongly advised not to attempt any changes in existing design or any new design without competent professional advice. Some of the more important steps are:

Reduce heating and cooling losses through building envelope

Cool with outside air whenever possible

Select lighting levels and lighting equipment for maximum conservation

Choose equipment that can operate at reduced loading without too much impairment of efficiency

Select equipment for maximum efficiency instead of for first cost (difficult to prove to an owner)

Design interior core area for cooling only and use heat gain for
perimeter areas

It may be difficult or financially impractical to change the systems
in a building built in the last 25 years or so because in many cases such
buildings contain reasonably adequate installations for heating, ventilation, electrical power, lighting, and plumbing. It could be considered
foolish to change duct sizes or replace still functioning boilers, fans, or
compressors unless new ones can save their cost in a short time. But
certainly new insulation, new lighting fixtures, and the recalculation of
heating and cooling loads with consequent changes in some duct runs,
fan capacities, and other equipment is completely practical. It is simpler to start new, as in an older underutilized building which contains
little if any modern installation.

9-4   SOME CONSTRUCTION GUIDELINES

The Building Envelope

THE EXTERIOR WALLS

Depending on its construction, the building envelope can conduct
from 10 to 20 percent of the total energy used by a building. The wide
variation proves how important proper construction and insulation can
be. The recycler cannot take full advantage of this because preservation
of the exterior of a building is a must in many successful recyclings, but
one of the great advantages of older buildings is that they were usually
much more substantially built than construction today. The exterior
walls are usually of masonry, which has thermal inertia. This means
that a rise or fall in exterior temperature will be transmitted slowly and
will allow the interior temperature to compensate for these temperature
swings in a gradual manner. This is a great energy saver. Thermal
inertia is most important in areas subject to long cold winters or long
hot summers with extreme temperature variations. The U value of
walls should be not more than 0.06 when winter design temperatures
are 10°F or less and 0.15 when winter design temperatures are above
40°F. For summer design U can vary from 0.06 in hot climates to 0.30
in moderate climates.

With the exterior walls already in place, the only way heat loss can
be reduced is by the use of insulation. Studies have shown that the best
location for insulation is outside the mass of the building. The mass of
the building then acts as a thermal storage area to further dampen the

interior temperature variations. Insulated metal panels fastened to the existing masonry not only give the building a modern appearance but act as extremely effective heat insulation. This method is expensive, however, and the next best method is by providing insulation on the interior side of the walls. Verminproof, rotproof material should be used, e.g., glass or rock wool or the plastics like styrofoam and urethane.[1] The architect should strive for the thickest insulation he can possibly afford and cover it with a furred wall. The more dead air space the better. He must not forget a vapor barrier on the warm side of the insulation. The materials that can be applied to the inside of an exterior wall like a plaster have limited insulating qualities and are subject to deterioration through dampness. The architect must make certain that the exterior walls are tight by having loose mortar joints repaired and by checking flashing and caulking.

WINDOWS AND DOORS

The openings in the exterior envelope of a structure are the greatest wasters of energy and the most difficult to control. They waste heat by conduction, radiation, and infiltration.

Heat loss through glass by conduction can be greatly decreased by double glazing. Tests show that in a climate equivalent to Chicago, which has an average of 6155 degree-days per year, double glazing (with its consequent dead air space) can save approximately 62,000 Btu per square foot of glass per year. Let us take a building with 100 windows each of 12 ft^2 for a total of 1200 ft^2. Such a building would save 74.4 million Btu per year by double glazing. This amounts to 540 gal of No. 2 oil or about $250 per year at 45 cents per gallon. It would cost about $2200 to provide 100 storm windows. This does not seem like a quick payoff of an investment, but as the cost of oil goes up, the savings will be larger and larger. Double glazing will also cut down on infiltration.

If the existing sash and frames cannot be used in the recycled building, the architect and owner should consider new double-glazed windows.

Infiltration through window and door openings can account for a very substantial loss of heat. Wind velocities and extreme difference in temperature between interior and exterior aggravate this loss. The obvious solutions are weatherstripping, gasketing of fixed glass, and caulking. Outside doors should be weatherstripped, preferably with metal interlocking weatherstripping. If space and expense permit, the installation of an unheated vestibule between exterior and interior

[1]The last two emit noxious fumes when heated.

doors is a great energy saver, as are self-closing door checks. Vertical shafts (stairways, elevators, and pipe and electrical shafts) act as flues and must be sealed. A simple precaution like having elevator machine-room doors and windows and stair bulkhead doors weatherstripped will help. In stairways and elevators this can be done by providing well-fitting self-closing doors. Pipe and electric shafts should be sealed at least at top and bottom. Wind breaks on ventilation louvers are another means of reducing infiltration.

If it is possible to cut down on the size of windows, the recycler should do so. Of course expense and architectural integrity should be considered. Most older buildings predating the "glass box" already have smaller windows.

Solar glare is another important consideration. Proper shading can help a great deal. This can be accomplished most economically by using venetian blinds, which can be adjusted to give the benefits of solar radiation in the cold months and to shield against it in the warm weather. Exterior sun shading in a recycled building is generally too expensive. If the building is small and has some greenery around it, awnings add an attractive touch.

THE ROOF

An exposed roof is a great source of heat loss in the cold months and is subject to all-day sun load in the summer. The answer is insulation and, if possible, dead air space. Two inches of rigid roof insulation laid over the old roof and covered with built-up roofing is recommended. If the roof surface is irregular, sprayed-on insulation covered with built-up roofing can also be used. An extra precaution is to provide blanket or blown-in insulation between the top floor ceiling and the underside of the roof. The saving for a small building 50 by 100 ft, or 5000 ft^2, located in an area with a climate the equivalent of Chicago is about $250 per year. The extra cost would be only for the insulation because the built-up roofing would undoubtedly be necessary in any case.

THE FLOOR

The only floor that need be considered is the bottom floor. It may be a slab on grade or built over a crawl space. In these cases insulation should be considered. If the perimeter of a slab on grade is insulated from the weather, this is all that can be hoped for. Over a cold crawl space, a 2-in blanket under the floor will cut the heat loss by at least 50 percent. A concrete floor slab can be insulated by sprayed-on insulating material.

In carrying out any of these energy-savings suggestions, the architect and the owner must always bear in mind that the work may have to be done later at greatly increased cost because public authority may order it.

Table 9-1 of U values for roof, walls, and floor in various climates is an indicator of the values that may eventually be imposed by code.

Interior Installations

PARTITIONING

Open space is much more efficient in the use of energy for heating, cooling, or lighting. If the building is being recycled for a specific user, perhaps the architect can point out that partitions less than ceiling high provide both visual privacy and greater efficiency. Ceiling-high partitions should be used only where necessary for both visual and audio privacy.

It is usual to have office or general working space located in the perimeter with the working core in the center. When it is possible to locate a corridor on an outside wall, this acts as a very good insulator against the changes in temperatures transmitted through an exterior wall.

LIGHTING

Lighting is a major consumer of electric energy. Many newer buildings have conspicuously exceeded any sensible lighting loads. The newest recommendation, based on studies of the amount of light required for

TABLE 9-1 SUGGESTED MINIMUM ROOF, WALL, AND FLOOR U VALUES, Btu/(h)(ft^2)(°F)

Heating degree-days	Roof		Wall	Floor	
	Roof-ceiling combination	Roof only*	Gross exterior-wall combination†	Above grade	On grade
0–3000	0.12	0.16	0.38		
3001–5000	0.10	0.14	0.34	0.13	0.26
5001–8000	0.06	0.10	0.30	0.10	0.20
8001 and above	0.04	0.08	0.27	0.08	0.20

*Exposed roof structure; no ceiling.

†Values are the sum of U values, proportioned by respective areas of opaque wall area, window area, and other areas, e.g., door area.

TABLE 9-2 RECOMMENDED LIGHT LEVELS

	Visual difficulty*	Design level, fc	Range, fc
Service or public area	. . . . .	15	12–18
Circulation areas in office space but not at work station	. . . . .	30	24–36
Normal office work, reading, writing, typing, etc.	1–39	50	40–60
Visually difficult office work, bookkeeping, drafting	40–59	75	60–90

*Visual difficulty is a number derived by multiplying the rating of a task by the number of hours it is performed. For instance, normal office work is rated between 4 and 5. If a secretary or stenographer types, reads shorthand, etc., for 7½ h, the visual difficulty is 4.5 × 7.5 = 33.7. For drafting or bookkeeping the rating is 8. Multiplying gives 8 × 7.5 h = 60.

various office tasks, is for an overall load factor of 2.3 W per square foot of net rentable area. This can be accomplished by choosing the most efficient luminaire, by keeping it clean (dirty fixtures and lamps can lose up to 30 percent of their efficiency), and by careful placement so that there is as much light and as little glare as possible. This last can be accomplished by skillful interior design. Whether a building is being recycled for general commercial rental or for a particular purpose for an owner or renter, the interior designer can arrange the lighting pattern so that the light source falls between tasks rather than directly over them. For the greatest efficiency lighting patterns should be laid out to suit the tasks on hand rather than for visual patterns where lighting fixtures are laid out in straight rows spaced the same distance apart without any regard to the tasks which are to be performed in their light. While this is not as neat, the owner or renter will appreciate the difference in his lighting bill and will know that the designer has been concerned with energy conservation.

Presently recommended light levels based on the nature of the work to be performed are shown in Table 9-2.

Although the recommended level of wiring capacity is for 2.3 W/ft², the designer will realize that tasks change and that buildings can be used for other purposes. He will therefore allow for extra capacity in his wiring design and for flexibility, e.g., when a typing pool is changed to a drafting room.

Figure 9-1 shows graphically how the wise choice of luminaires adds to the efficiency of the lighting. Note that the use of a direct fluorescent luminaire with a lens (K) requires only 2.3 W/ft² to produce 50 fc.

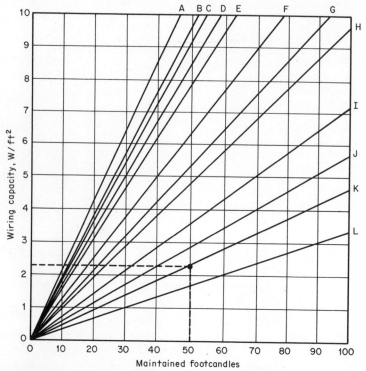

Maintained footcandles

FIGURE 9-1 Approximate wiring capacity to provide a given maintained level of illumination in a room with room cavity ratio of 2.5: *A*, indirect, incandescent filament (silvered bowl); *B*, direct, incandescent filament (with diffuser); *C*, direct, incandescent filament; *D*, general diffuse, incandescent filament; *E*, direct, incandescent filament (lens); *F*, direct, incandescent filament (industrial) or indirect, fluorescent (cove); *G*, indirect, fluorescent (extra-high output); *H*, direct, fluorescent (extra-high output, louvered); *I*, direct, fluorescent (louvered); *J*, luminous ceiling, fluorescent; *K*, direct, fluorescent (lens) or HID (mercury); and *L*, direct semidirect, fluorescent (industrial).

The Mechanical Systems

HEATING AND COOLING

The central plant The first consideration in reducing the heating and cooling load is obviously proper insulation of the building exterior (Sec. 9-4). When this important matter has been attended to, the next step is to cut down on the loss of efficiency in the heating and cooling central plants and distribution. If new central plants are to be installed, there are many devices for increasing their efficiency. The design of the plants should take into account the design criteria on summer cooling and winter heating.

Winter: 68°F dry-bulb temperature

Summer: 78°F dry-bulb with 65 percent relative humidity

The sizing of the plants should also take into consideration heat gain from body heat when the building is occupied and reduced heating and cooling when the building is unoccupied. Refrigeration systems should be shut down during unoccupied periods.

If the structure is too small to warrant the installation of a flue-gas analyzer, the next best thing is to provide a test kit for checking boiler efficiency or to advise the owner or occupant (whoever pays for the fuel) to do so.

The fuel to be used is strictly a matter of what is available now and in the future and its probable cost in various regions of the country. The use of coal as fuel is not out of the question. Solar heating is a bit far off, but possibly some inexpensive provisions can be made for it now.

The distribution system   The insulation of piping and ductwork is very important. The architect-engineer should see to this whether it is to be installed on new or existing piping. For instance, an uninsulated 1½-in pipe carrying 200°F water will lose about 2700 Btu/h whereas even ½ in of insulation will cut this down to 250 Btu. The insulation of the ductwork is also important. A duct without insulation that carries air at a 30°F difference will lose 30 Btu/(h)(ft²), while ½ in of insulation will cut this down to 17 Btu and 1 in will further reduce it to 7 Btu.

VENTILATION

The amount of ventilation to be provided is usually regulated by the building code. There are some criteria, however, which can be of help. Usually a supply of 1 to 2 ft³/min per person is sufficient for normal office work areas. For areas with some smoking or light odors this should be increased up to 4 ft³/min.

The most saving can be obtained by selective ventilation of particular areas such as kitchen or laboratories. The use of excessive outdoor air is also discouraged. There are seasons in many regions of the country when 100 percent outdoor air can be used. Usually, however, it has to be heated or cooled, which uses more energy than recycling the indoor air with some make-up from the outdoors.

PLUMBING

Domestic hot water at 105°F is satisfactory and should be supplied during working hours at a rate of 1½ gal/day per person. Shut-off controls should be installed to turn the heating off during unoccupied hours.

Drinking water (if refrigerated) should not be lower than 55°F and shut-off controls should be installed. Many good office buildings of all sizes and in all parts of the country do not have public drinking fountains, refrigerated or not.

Existing laboratory faucets should be of automatic-shut-off type. Water is becoming both scarce and expensive in many regions, and we all are aware of people who leave hot or cold water running at full force even when it is not in use. There are also many ways of using waste heat from condensate returns, from water-cooled compressors or gas engines, etc., to heat domestic hot water.

VERTICAL TRANSPORTATION

When a building with elevators is recycled, the architect should look closely to determine whether any elevators can be eliminated even though waiting time is somewhat increased. High-speed high-capacity elevators consume much more energy than slower ones and cost more to install. Selection of slower elevators is especially useful for buildings under eight or ten stories. Worm-geared and hydraulic elevators are very economical. Escalators should be used only in high-density transportation. They are large energy users.

9-5 BUILDING MANAGEMENT FOR ENERGY CONSERVATION

When the recycling team has completed the reconstruction of the building and has, within economic limits, completed the installation of all the materials and equipment recommended for the conservation of energy, the next step is to maintain the building in such a manner that the cost of these installations will not have been wasted.

If the recycling has been for an owner, he will certainly appreciate what has been done for his profitable future ownership. If the recyclers are doing it for their own account, they will reap the future benefits and avoid any retroactive governmental demands.

Setting a Goal

The first step in setting a goal is determining the energy used in a base year, which should be the first year of full normal operation. Even if the recyclers will not be owning the building, it is recommended that they

TABLE 9-3 SUMMARY OF ENERGY USE

Month	Heating degree-days	Cooling degree-days	kWh	Demand, kW	Electrical Total cost	Electrical Btu (gross ft²) (degree-day)
Jan.						
Feb.						
etc.						

Month	Heating degree-days	Cooling degree-days	Oil, no.——, gal	Cost	Natural gas, 1000 ft³	Fuel cost	Coal, Tons	Cost	Btu/(gross ft²)(degree-day)
Jan.									
Feb.									
etc.			.						

instruct the owner or operator of the building how to do this. It is not too much trouble and can lead to return or recommended new business. A simple table (Table 9-3) can be prepared so that the building operator can see exactly how his energy dollar was spent. He can also see how his energy use has gone up or come down because of maintenance or because of the possible addition of energy-saving devices as the building begins to pay off. In Table 9-3 all energy is reduced to Btu in accordance with the values in Table 9-4. The origin and composition of the coal must be determined. Tables of Btu values for various coals are available in handbooks. The summary of energy use (Table 9-3) should be kept on a monthly basis. Electrical and fuel energy summa-

TABLE 9-4 EQUIVALENT BTU VALUES FOR DIFFERENT ENERGY SOURCES

Source	Btu
Electricity, 1 kWh	3,413
Steam, 1 lb	1,200
Natural gas, 1 ft³	1,000
Fuel oil, 1 gal:	
No. 2	138,000
No. 6	148,000
Coal, 1 lb	Use 10,000–14,000

ries are kept separately to make it easier to find where energy can be saved and how the proper maintenance or changing equipment helps.

Maintenance of Building and Equipment

USE OF SPACE[1]

Try to place all heat-producing equipment (copying machines) in one space; try to place all computers or computer-type equipment in one space.

Close off unused areas.

Keep furniture and wall hangings away from supply or return ducts and from perimeter heating or cooling.

Avoid, if possible, ceiling-high partitions..

BUILDING ENVELOPE

Check window and door weatherstripping and caulking at regular intervals.

Install venetian blinds and give instructions for their proper use in cold and warm weather.

Place automatic door checks on exterior doors and keep them in good operating order.

Instruct occupants not to open windows while building is being heated or cooled.

If garage is in building, check to be sure that entrance doors are kept closed (automatic operator activated by treadles).

If there is no vestibule at the front entrance, consider installation of one when affordable.

VENTILATION AND AIR HANDLING

Inspect all outside dampers for air leakage.

Limit outside air to minimum required to balance exhaust system plus a small positive pressure.

---

[1]This is for an owner-occupied building. Owners cannot usually control tenants' use of space.

Reduce exhaust air to minimum required.

In a small building the toilet light may be wired to a fan so that exhaust is used only when toilet is occupied.

Use exhaust hoods in cooking areas only when food is being prepared.

Check fans for noise and vibration.

Inspect and lubricate bearings on a regular basis.

Check filters for cleanliness on a regular basis.

Keep fan blades clean.

Check fan belts for slippage.

Check motor alignments.

Lubricate motor and drive bearings on a regular basis.

Inspect ducts for leakage. Inspect damper blades and linkages.

REFRIGERATION

Check all compressor joints for leakage.

Continuously check oil pressure and temperature.

Check compressor for excessive vibration or frequent stopping and starting.

Condensers: keep coils clean, check fan belt, and check for tight joints.

Cooling tower: keep clean, use water treatment, check fan, and clean strainers.

Self-contained units: keep filters and louvers clean and caulk opening between window and unit.

HEATING EQUIPMENT

Boiler: inspect water side for scale and sediment and fire side for fly ash, soot, and slag; inspect door gaskets; check stack emission for complete combustion; check for boiler efficiency (O_2, CO, CO_2) and stack temperature; check refractory brick work; check boiler insulation.

Distribution: check pipe insulation; keep grilles and filters of heating units clean; check valves.

PLUMBING

Inspect all water lines for leaks; check hot-water-line insulation.

Inspect insulation on storage tanks.

Turn off hot-water circulating pump when building is unoccupied.

Keep water at 105°F maximum.

Consider installation of pressure-reducing valves to cut down on water flow.

ELECTRICAL

Encourage building personnel to turn off all power-using equipment when not in use, e.g., fans, typewriters, coffee makers, calculators.

Keep electrical control rooms clean and dry and ventilated to prevent heat buildup.

Demand management: demand charges are a very important part of the cost of electricity. Avoid simultaneous operation of heavy power-consuming equipment. Use timing devices for compressors, fire pumps, ventilating fans, cooling-tower fans, circulating pumps, etc.

Lighting: keep fixtures clean. Replace yellowed lenses. Check light output with a calibrated light meter. When level of lighting is 70 percent or less of designed level, all lamps in an area should be changed at the same time. Keep lights turned off in rooms not in use.

MAINTENANCE IN GENERAL

The maintenance suggestions mentioned above are only the more important ones. There are dozens of others that a good maintenance man will find if he is properly indoctrinated. Most of these suggestions will cost very little to carry out.

9-6   ADDITIONAL ENERGY-SAVING DEVICES

Unlike maintenance procedures, the following suggestions will cost money to carry out, but if they save their cost in 5 years or less, they will be worthwhile. They should not be considered without a cost study, and most of them require engineering advice.

The addition of an unheated or uncooled vestibule at the front entrance has already been suggested. This is a great saver of energy because the trapped air in the vestibule acts as a very effective insulator. Revolving doors perform the same function, but since they are not legal exits, doors will have to be provided as well.

The addition of storm windows has been suggested. Reflective double glazing is expensive but very efficient. Reflective glazing will cut down to some extent on natural lighting.

The heating and cooling systems are usually balanced before the building is occupied or immediately thereafter. Rebalancing the system after some months of normal operation can result in uncovering trouble spots and in a general lowering of the need for heating or cooling.

The wastage of water, both hot and cold, has been discussed. Spring or spray-type faucets with flow restrictors are recommended.

It is not always easy in the original design to locate luminaires where they will be most efficient. Relocating luminaires after the work patterns have been established and consideration of special lenses in problem areas are suggested. Such lenses can save the expense of additional luminaires. Expert advice is needed.

Again these are only a few of the many things that can be done to save energy. The need to save energy is one of the most important issues facing the country today.

FINAL PLANS

AND

SPECIFICATIONS

10-1 THE SPECIAL NATURE OF PLANS AND SPECIFICATIONS FOR RECYCLING

The word "recycling" means to "return for further use." In the recycling process there is always an existing structure. The structure may be old or almost new. The new use may be the same as the old, or it may be so completely different that the original designer could have had no idea that the existing structure would be adapted to such a use.

In ordinary new construction the plans and specifications follow a fixed sequence, and since everything is new, the construction process also follows a sequence in which certain installations are completed before others can be started. This is true in recycling. Sometimes a number of different installations are going on at the same time. The architect-engineer must therefore prepare a set of plans and specifications which will define as closely as possible which portion of the existing structure is to be demolished, which is to remain to be reused, and which is to be new. To some extent he must guide the sequence in which these things are done.

Summary of the Necessary Contents

It is recommended that all recycling specifications follow the same fixed sequence, enabling the owner and the contractor to find each trade in its proper place and assuring the architect that nothing has been omitted. The construction industry and various organizations of architects, engineers, and others formulated a construction index consisting of 16 sections. Since most architects and engineers use this sequence, all the parties to the construction know where to look for what.

Each trade specification in this chapter will be preceded by a general note, which is in the nature of a general conditions section but which applies only to the specific requirements of that trade. The architect or engineer who writes the specifications is aware, of course, that in construction in general the various subcontractors must work as a team. Unfortunately this does not always happen, and many subcontractors will try to slough off as much as they can of any collateral work like patching or cleaning up, etc. The result may be that the general contractor or the owner finally pays. This can be particularly so in recycling, where the point at which one subcontractor takes over from another is sometimes ill defined. This special general conditions section is written to eliminate this conflict insofar as possible.

The following trade specifications have been taken from a number of actual specifications used in the construction of various buildings. Their purpose here is to serve as a checklist for recyclers who must be able to save some existing equipment, masonry, structure, etc., and use new material in order to assemble a complete functioning structure.

Specifications vary to some extent at the beginning, some architects simply inserting the General Conditions Form of AIA at the start and placing supplemental and special conditions under Section 1. Others start the specifications by inserting an entire Section 0 before the actual work is defined. This seems less confusing and is recommended.

Conditions of the Contract

GENERAL CONDITIONS

These are usually the AIA Document mentioned above.

SUPPLEMENTARY GENERAL CONDITIONS

The standard general conditions are necessarily very broad because they must apply to all kinds of construction. It is through the supplementary conditions that the owner and the architect can alter these standards so that they will meet their own requirements. For instance under "insurance" the owner will insert his own requirements for the kind of insurance and for the amount of coverage. Under "cutting and patching of work" one architect has inserted the following:

> Each section of the specifications describes the cutting, patching, digging, etc., required for the work under that section as may be required for the proper accommodation of that and other trades. This does not relieve the general contractor or any subcontractor from the responsibility as shown in the general conditions.

This clause is particularly important in recycling work. The architect has defined what each subcontractor must do for himself and for others. This can eliminate a great deal of dispute between subcontractors. But in recycling work existing work is often added to or unforeseen conditions are often found, and there are times when the responsibility for the necessary cutting and patching is ill defined. The architect therefore gives the general contractor the final overall responsibility for seeing that all such work is done.

There are other sections of the general conditions the architect or owner may want to change. The progress schedule may have to be specially defined for a recycling project because some installations may have to be made out of sequence. It also allows the architect to choose the kind of progress schedule he requires (critical path or bar chart).

SPECIAL CONDITIONS

The special conditions are often used to call the contractor's particular attention to work that must be done but which may fall between the trades or which may be missed by the contractor or his subcontractors in the trade specifications. For instance, a special condition may state, "Access to existing business shall be maintained at all times. Contractor shall provide all necessary fencing, warning signs, lights, and temporary protection." Or "The contractor shall provide a capable dependable watchman, or watchmen in shifts as may be deemed necessary, to guard the construction and materials stored at the site." Or the special conditions may contain a description of the authority and duties of a resident engineer. The special conditions can also be specific about any peculiar requirements for temporary protection, temporary heat, or other temporary facilities.

ADDENDA

The addenda to a specification serve to modify the plans and specifications after they have been drawn or written. In a recycling project the architect may find conditions that were not evident in his initial inspection, or the owner may require an installation that was not originally contemplated. A contractor or subcontractor who is bidding the job may find that he cannot perform according to the original specifications. The architect-engineer can use the addenda for adding and deleting work from any section of the specification.

GENERAL REQUIREMENTS

Some architects use a general-requirements clause at the beginning of each section of the specification to describe what is expected of the contractor for that particular trade. Others use a general-requirements section to set the conditions for the entire work. Such requirements contain standard headings such as "work included," which mention demolition and salvage, "responsibility and intent," "examination of conditions," etc.

Alternates   While many architects and owners place their request for alternate prices in the bid-proposal form, others will list these alternates in the general-requirements section. Alternates, especially in a recycling, must be very carefully considered. It is essential that a price be set for every possible major contingency and that this price be set during the bidding period, when every contractor is doing his best to obtain the award. A typical case is anticipation of tenant requirements for structural changes. In one case the architect asked for an alternate for an entirely new roof including decking, insulation, and roofing. There may be alternates for sound isolation, for special insulation such as double windows, or for placement of an air-conditioning or heating installation in the basement or on the roof.

Unit prices   It is also advantageous for the architect to ask for unit prices at bid time for any anticipated work. The writer has seen requests for unit prices on larger projects that may number well over 100 items. This is not usually necessary, but the architect should anticipate items that will certainly come up, e.g.,

Mass rock excavation, per cubic yard

Trench rock excavation, per cubic yard

Pier-hole rock excavation, per cubic yard

Metal stud partition, 8 ft high,

½-in gypsum board, two sides, per linear foot

1¾-in solid-core wood door (describe hardware and finish), per door

1¾-in hollow-core wood door (describe hardware and finish), per door

Shelving, cabinetwork, drinking fountains, floor tile, etc.

10-2 SITE WORK

Site work embraces all the operations necessary to prepare the site for the necessary reconstruction called for by the recycling program. The following list is a sample of the various processes involved:

Demolition and removal of existing site work and preparation for required new work

Excavating, filling, and grading for new work

Fill for new slabs on ground

Backfilling

Protection of existing utilities

Pumping and draining of excavation

Furnishing, erecting, and maintaining fencing, signs, etc., for protecting the excavation

Removing all excess excavated material, rubbish, and debris

Temporary shoring, sheet piling, and bracing

Excavation

This specification should include:

1. A general note that states that test borings, soil reports, etc., are for reference only and that the contractor may make his own investigations at his own expense if he wishes to verify any conditions; a note that the contractor accepts the site "as is."

2. The general requirements for any excavation such as the stepping of rock slopes, the digging for footings to firm undisturbed soil or other material that has the required bearing capacity, the placement of fill in cases where the excavation must go below the required finish grade, the stockpiling of top soil, etc.

General Site Work

This includes all exterior work that could be called landscaping. It includes top-soiling, seeding and fertilizer, planting, paving for vehicles and pedestrians, concrete curbs and walks, bituminous curbs and walks, traffic marking, storm-water piping, catch basins, and manholes.

10-3   CAST-IN-PLACE CONCRETE

The specification for this trade should include a general note that all concrete must be prepared to a design mix and must be tested by a recognized testing laboratory. It should also include a requirement for certificates of quality of reinforcing steel.

The work should include reinforcing, footings, basement floor slabs, grade beams, form work, covering of existing floors with concrete fill, machine foundations, reinforcing of areas for machine rooms for air conditioning and heating, elevator pits and elevator machine rooms, grouting of iron and steel work, concrete roof fill, balconies, lintels, stairs, and landings.

A partial list of some of the materials that are usually specified would include vapor barriers for on-grade slabs, various admixtures for retarding or accelerating setting, abrasive aggregates, floor hardeners, premolded joint fillers, bond breakers, and anchor slots.

The specification should also contain explicit directions for placing the concrete, curing, cold-weather placement, protection of concrete, and removal of forms.

10-4   MASONRY

The specification for masonry for recycling work should include all brickwork, blockwork, flue-tile work, fire brick, anchoring and bonding of masonry, furring and building chases, cutting and patching of existing masonry, and altering and adding to existing masonry.

In recycling work it is important that the masonry contractor coordinate his work with other trades (especially the mechanical trades) so that he can cut openings through walls or floors exactly when and where they are required. Another clause that is important in recycling is the salvaging and reuse of brick and the importance of color- and texture-matching exterior brick.

The specification should also include the standard requirements for any masonry work such as anchors and ties, control joints, masonry reinforcement, weepholes, and types of mortar.

In all work, new or old, the building code will call for masonry partitions to run the full height of a floor, for wall ties and masonry reinforcement at certain specified points, for firesafing around all openings for mechanical or other work in fire walls, for strength of material, etc.

10-5   METALS

Structural Steel and Steel Joists

The design and the specifications for structural steel in recycling require particular care. Most structures recycled to bring them up to modern standards require structural reinforcement because of (1) the modern code requirements, e.g., for stairs and exits; (2) the additional mechanical and electrical work required to bring a structure up to present-day standards, which means that new openings have to be cut in floors and walls and must be reinforced; (3) framing for a new elevator or elevators; and (4) new heavy equipment, e.g., air-conditioning and heating units, fans, or unit heaters, which must be supported by steel. All this new structural steel must be fitted in and coordinated with the existing structure and must not only support the new work but in many cases act as a support for the existing structure. Open-web steel joists are used a great deal for new floors or reinforcing floors in recycling.

The quality of the material and workmanship is the same for recycling as for new work.

Metal Decking

In recycling it is often more practical to replace a portion of a floor or an entire floor than to attempt to repair it. Sometimes one or more entire new floors are added. A practical and not too expensive way of doing this is by using steel decking over steel girders and joists. It is very quickly installed and provides a secure floor for workers. A number of companies manufacture this decking, which comes in several forms. All such decking must conform with ASTM and code standards.

The specifications for quality and workmanship are the same as those for all new construction.

Miscellaneous Metals

This section is a catch-all for all metal work on the job except for items specifically included in sections of their own. Not all the work included in this section need be done by the same subcontractor and very often it is not. A sample of the work usually included in miscellaneous metals follows:

Steel-pan stairs, platforms, landings, and railings

Metal saddles for exterior and interior door openings

Lintels for masonry openings

Ladders, gratings, elevator-shaft openings

Aluminum railings, louvers

Cooling-tower enclosures

All shop prime coating and field touch-up painting

In residential recyclings fireplace equipment, closet rods, or balcony framing and railing

10-6   ROUGH CARPENTRY AND FRAMING

In some specifications the architect separates rough carpentry and framing from finish carpentry and millwork. Others combine them. The choice depends on the amount of structural wood framing involved. In the specification quoted here a wall-bearing heavy mill-type structure was involved. The work included the following:

All floor repairs and infills using salvaged or new beams

Plywood or matchboard flooring to match height of existing floors

Notching of beams and cutting and heading for soil pipes, ducts, etc.

All necessary strapping and blocking to reinforce existing structure

All temporary protection, ladders, runways, etc.

All rough hardware

Roof sheathing and nailers for flashing

Finish Carpentry and Millwork

Although the title of the section is finish carpentry, some rough carpentry is necessarily involved even though under this section it would be relatively minor. Following is a sample of the work normally included in this category. It will be noted that there are overlaps.

All rough carpentry work where shown on drawings including, but not limited to, grounds, blocking, nailers, rough frames or bricks, furring, etc.

All wood doors and frames

Folding partitions and trim

Counters, cabinets (including wall cabinets, base cabinets, sink cabinets), and countertops

Shelving and paneling

Kitchen cabinets and counters

Wood railing and handrails

Window trim, baseboards, miscellaneous trim

Installing hollow metal doors and frames, including hardware (sometimes furnished by others)

Installing bathroom accessories (furnished by others)

The quality and workmanship portion of the specification mentions such items as wood preservative for exposed wood, the quality of the lumber and millwork, and the quality and material of the cabinetwork, the paneling, and other finish woodwork.

10-7   MOISTURE AND THERMAL PROTECTION

Roofing and Sheet Metal

In most recycling an important part of the work is replacing a deteriorated roof. The architect should take good care that the specifications for the roofing and sheet metal are for the best quality possible.

Built-up roofing should be of the quality and workmanship that could qualify for a 20-year bond. Flashing material should be of the copper-reinforced type fabric, dead-soft stainless steel, copper-clad metal aluminum, or copper-clad stainless steel. A built-up slag roof should have a gravel surfacing of from 300 to 400 lb of material per 100 ft².

Attention must be paid to the secure and proper attachment of the flashing to the roofing and parapet walls by means of cant strips and reglets. It often happens in recycling that two or more structures originally under separate ownership are joined under a common roof. In such a case the joining must be done very carefully. The following is from a specification:

> Where new and existing built-up roofing adjoins, the gravel or slag surfacing shall be removed from the existing roofing for a width of 12 in and new roofing felts shall extend over the existing in four plies of 6-, 8-, 10-, and 12-in widths. Gravel or slag surfacing shall be applied in a flood coat of hot pitch.

Attention should also be paid to necessary expansion joints.

Building Insulation

ROOF INSULATION

Roof insulation usually consists of blocks of compressed glass fiber, foamed glass, or rigid foamed polyurethane board, which in turn are covered by the built-up waterproof roofing. On metal decks the specification should call for setting the board in hot pitch mopped on the ridges or on ribbon applications of an adhesive. On flat roofs it is laid in hot pitch, and on sloped roofs it must be held by suitable fasteners to prevent slippage. The new code requirements for thermal insulation will set the thickness of the board.

BUILDING INSULATION (THERMAL)

Most older buildings have little or no wall insulation, which must be provided in the recycling. Most of such insulation is specified to be at least 4-in-thick batts of mineral or glass wool set between furring strips and adhered to the outer wall by adhesive. The architect should also consider insulation under the first floor when there is unheated space under it or under the roof as an addition to the rigid roof insulation.

Caulking

All caulking in older buildings should be replaced. Existing caulking that may look good to the casual eye may have lost its elasticity and waterproofing quality. The best thing to do is to rake it out and replace it.

Caulking is applied at masonry expansion joints, around windows and door openings, at the tops of roof reglets, at any pipe sleeves and ducts that penetrate exterior surfaces, at joints between concrete block and brick, and at any other point where there is a chance of moisture penetration.

10-8   DOORS, WINDOWS, AND GLASS

Hollow Metal

Older buildings usually contain wood door frames and doors and wood sash. In many cases the lack of preservative measures has left such window frames and sash too far gone to be reused. Even if they are in good condition, they cannot be used in party-line walls or in any situation which conflicts with modern fire codes. The architect then has the choice of steel or aluminum windows of many styles (sliding, awning, double-hung, stationary, casement, etc.).

Steel windows should be of cold-rolled furniture-steel quality and aluminum windows of extruded tubular-type construction. All metal sash doors and bucks have to be prefinished by bonderizing or an equal process.

Steel doors and pressed-steel frames (or bucks) are of cold-rolled steel and aluminum doors and frames are of tubular construction extrusions. All metal windows, doors, and frames must be factory-prepared to receive hardware, and the architect must be particularly careful about shop drawings. All fire doors must be of underwriter-labeled metal construction.

Wood Windows

The writer knows of several recyclings in which most of the existing wood windows and frames, especially in the front elevation, have been in a good state of preservation. In these cases the architect has specified new wood windows and frames to match the existing ones. This preserves the architectural style, which is one of the selling points of recycling old buildings.

Glazing

A concern of the architect in a recycling operation is matching new glass with the existing glass, especially where a good deal of old window glass remains in well-preserved sash. The architect can place the new glass in places where it cannot be immediately compared with the old glass from the *interior*. The standards of strength for new glass are a function of the size of the light. This is not always so in old glass.

Many architects are using double glazing in recyclings in order to conform to the new energy-saving standards and to save fuel cost. With the continually rising cost of fuel it is becoming more economical to install double glazing and other energy-saving devices.

Finish Hardware

This item of work is usually specified as an allowance. Some architects, however, specify a complete hardware list by manufacturer, size, and catalog number and leave it to the contractor to obtain bids. This of course ties the architect to a specific product and design, which may not be as economical in a recycling project because all kinds of unexpected extra hardware may be required with consequent change orders involved.

10-9   FINISHES

Furring, Lath, and Plaster

Today most walls and ceilings are of gypsum board or acoustic tile (in ceilings). A considerable amount of furring and plastering can be involved, especially if steel or heavy timber bracing is required and if old corners need to be covered. This trade is also used for lathing and vermiculite plastering over boiler or service rooms, for certain exposed soffits, for closing holes through fire walls, for lathing to hold plasterboard ceilings, and for any other miscellaneous patch jobs.

Dry Wall

Gypsum dry wall is used to cover the inside of exterior walls, to face interior partitions, to provide finished ceilings, to provide fireproof enclosures for elevator shafts, fire stairs, and corridors, to box in ducts and piping, and wherever else the architect finds it feasible to use this material, which is cheaper to install than lath and plaster.

Gypsum board in fire-rated buildings is installed over galvanized-metal studs and runners that are usually manufactured by the supplier of the board. Fire-rated board is strictly defined by local code. Many localities of any size have subcontractors who specialize in erecting and finishing gypsum-board dry wall. Unless union or other rules interfere, the use of these contractors is recommended.

Many recycling projects use fire-resistant asphalt-impregnated gypsum board for exterior sheathing.

Acoustical Ceilings

Any building that is being recycled for office use is almost obligated to use acoustic hung ceilings in the office area. The hung ceiling serves to conceal ducts, electrical lines, and other services and in many cases can be used as a plenum chamber for return air. The hung ceiling is also used to conceal the upper portion of ceiling fixtures so that they appear flush with the finished ceiling.

Acoustic ceilings come in many patterns, and there are several modes of construction. The design that seems most prevalent in recyclings consists of fire-rated exposed tee bars on 24- by 48-in centers into which are laid acoustic mineral-fiber fire-rated lay-in panels of the same size. This also enables the architect to specify 24- by 48-in lighting fixtures carrying four 4-ft fluorescent tubes, which is the most economical size for a fluorescent.

In a recycling the architect must be particularly careful about the placement and fastening of the supporting hangers. The methods of fastening in existing floor construction and new floors may be totally different. This should be carefully pointed out in the plans and the specifications.

Ceramic Tile

Ceramic tile is generally used as a finish in toilet rooms and is more common in apartment recycling than in buildings for offices or other public use. There are many substitutes for ceramic tile, but they look like substitutes. This use of ceramics is well worth while in any structure which has to appeal to the public and which has to be maintained in good condition for many years. Floor and wall tile are set in adhesives, which cuts tile-setting time down to a minimum. Architects have a choice of size, color, and pattern, but the lead time for such choices must be carefully established. Ceramics are often used (and most attractively) in the walls and floors of selected public spaces.

Resilient Flooring

Resilient flooring is the usual floor covering in commercial buildings; it may also be used in residential recycling in corridors and other public spaces and in kitchens or bathrooms. The usual surfacing in office space or public spaces is vinyl asbestos. Floor covering in kitchens or baths should be linoleum or vinyl (which is expensive). Some residential recyclers use resilient tile in the living areas. It is much cheaper than wood flooring, but it is not recommended for any recycling project which makes any pretense to elegance.

Painting and Decorating

In this trade the architect has wide discretion in his use of materials and methods of application. There can be wall coverings; paints of various colors, materials, and textures; trowelled-on finishes; etc. He must always keep in mind durability and ease of maintenance.

Specialties

Toilet partitions, toilet accessories, medicine cabinets, mirrors, sink and basin cabinets, and built-ins of various other kinds are included in this specification category. Some of these items may have to be quoted as an allowance until the architect or owner has decided on what he wants, but specific provisions should be made in the various trade specifications to have them installed.

10-10   ELEVATORS

Any recycling of almost any kind that is over two stories high should have an elevator. This does not mean that the tenant or visitor to a recycled building expects to be wafted aloft by the latest in gearless elevators with collective selective controls and seven traffic patterns. It does mean that the architect can choose a slow-speed geared elevator with automatic door controls and collective floor signaling.

10-11   HEATING, VENTILATING, AND AIR CONDITIONING

General Note

The first entry in this note should state what work is *not* included in this trade and is included in work by others. This should be carefully written to make sure that the cost for the work is not duplicated in several trade bids.

An especially important clause for recycling states that the subcontractor must examine the premises carefully for existing conditions before submitting his bid. Any later claim for extras or unforeseen work will not be allowed.

Although most specifications carry a clause about their intent, it is especially important to state this clearly in a mechanical section as follows: "It is the intent of these specifications to provide complete systems, left in good working order, ready for operation, including necessary labor and materials, whether or not specifically shown on the drawings or mentioned herein."

To further clarify the intent a clause can be added: "Confer with others engaged in the construction . . . whose work might affect the installation and arrange all parts of the work and equipment in proper relation to the work and equipment of others. . . ."

Several other clauses should be inserted in the general notes as follows:

1. Furnish "as-built" drawings when work is completed. This is especially important in recycling, where existing and new work may be combined.

2. Perform all tests required by all the authorities having jurisdiction.

3. The proposal for work in any occupied area of the building shall be predicated on the performance of the work during regular working hours except where the specification indicates otherwise.

4. Remove or relocate, as called for on the drawings, existing equipment, piping, and fittings. Where pipe branches are indicated to be removed, they shall be removed back to the sections which shall remain. The contractor is to check each indicated junction point carefully for corrosion and its ability to withstand the new pressures and stresses that will be put upon it.

Piping, Valves, and Fittings

This section of the specifications for new construction can be used for a recycling specification with little change. The architect-engineer must remember that his completed building must comply with present codes. This means that all existing piping and fittings as well as the new must comply. The specification should also lay particular stress on cutting holes for piping through floors and walls before their completion. The contractor should be required to furnish a valve chart to show the location and function of every valve, existing or new. The architect-engineer should also be aware that pipes of dissimilar metals should not be used in the same line.

Pipe materials   Nickel-copper-alloy steel (YOLOY); copper tubing type K or L and hard- or soft-drawn, fittings solder type or brazed; steel pipe ANSI B36-10, fittings cast iron screw-type to 2½ in and steel butt-welded 3 in and over; victualic couplings and fittings where allowed by code; galvanized steel.

Auxiliary equipment   Hangers, sleeves, escutcheons, roller supports, expansion joints, access doors, anchors to structure, motorized valves, and chain operation for inaccessible valves, traps, and strainers.

Tests   Fill system with water, plug all openings, and subject to approved test pressure for 2 h.

Cleaning and treating   Piping, boilers, and equipment must be cleaned before using.

General Equipment

Radiation   Select copper tubes or steel pipe, copper fins, or aluminum fins. All enclosures to be of 18-gauge furniture steel with 12-gauge braces, coated with two coats of rust-resistant paint.

Heat exchangers   For hot-water heating or domestic hot water; select fuel for heating boiler (gas, fuel oil, electricity, heat pump); select type of boiler and hot-water generator.

Pumps   Select pumps for condensate and vacuum and fuel oil (where used).

Tanks   Fuel oil, expansion tank, compression tank, and air compressor.

Sheet-Metal Work

Scope   Remove existing ductwork as indicated on the drawings and provide new ductwork as called for by this specification and the drawings or wherever necessary to make a complete workable system.

Duct materials   Galvanized iron, black iron, stainless steel, or copper. Select gauges of metal depending on unsupported lengths, fire resistance, and use. Boiler breeching of $\frac{3}{16}$-in steel plate with welded seams. Flange connections with asbestos gaskets.

Dampers   Airflow dampers with quadrants to indicate position. Fire dampers with fusible links and underwriters labels, as called for by code. All fire dampers to have access doors. Special installation for a fire damper located in a fire wall. Smoke-detection heads.

Registers, grilles, and ceiling diffusers   Supply register, return and exhaust register, ceiling diffuser, linear supply diffuser, linear return grille, and transfer grille. A schedule of grilles, registers, and diffusers should be part of the plan to avoid omissions and for quick checking.

Acoustical treatment   Duct liners, turning vanes, prefabricated duct silencers.

Firesafing   Provide for firesafing in accordance with code of all ducts, pipes, etc., which pass through floors or fire walls.

System balancing   This is very important and should be included in the specifications and in the bid price. In any but the simplest jobs the services of a specialist in air balancing is suggested.

Ventilation Equipment

Filters   Throwaway panel filters; cartridge filters (permanent frame and replacement filters) of various efficiencies 50, 85, and 95 percent, rigid ultrahigh; mechanical automatic-roll type, two-stage roll-cartridge; grease filters; activated carbon filters; activated alumina or odoroxidant filters; side-loading filter assemblies.

Heating and cooling coils   For reheat or booster cooling in special areas (very expensive to operate). Electric or hot-water heating and cold-water cooling.

Fans   All blades to be of airfoil type. All fans to have varipitch sheave, V-belt drives, or adjustable inlet vanes; roof-type exhaust fans; package-type air-handling units; fan-coil units; unit heaters.

Auxiliary equipment   Thermostats, fan guards, belt drives, and moisture eliminators.

Special handling   For computer and other critical areas.

Refrigeration

Refrigeration equipment   To consist of steam- or electric-driven centrifugal or reciprocating compressor, direct-expansion chiller, refrigerant condenser, water cooler, purge recovery unit, controls, piping, bases, vibration isolation, and all accessories. Absorption refrigeration machine to consist of absorber, evaporator, concentrator, condenser, solution heat exchanger, solution pump, absorber pump, evaporator pump, purge system, and controls.

Safety control panel   To be located at each compressor unit and to contain cutouts for low oil pressure, low refrigerant temperature, high refrigerant-condenser pressure, low chilled-water temperature, plus various gauges, a starter button, and a control to ensure no-load starting of compressor.

Refrigerant condensers and cooling water   Refrigerant condensers can be air- or water-cooled. In smaller units they can be air-cooled. For larger units the engineer will usually specify a cooling tower. The cooling tower must be sprinkled and must contain a heating coil for use in sudden temperature drops in cooler latitudes.

Boiler Plant

The boiler plant can be used to produce high-pressure steam for steam turbines and for transfer heating of space and domestic hot water, low-pressure steam for heating and heat transfer for domestic hot water, or forced hot water for heating and domestic hot water. Boilers can be fire-tube, water-tube, or packaged horizontal-fire-tube Scotch marine type.

Fuel   Depending on availability and cost, fuel can be natural gas, fuel oil no. 2, 4, or 6, or electricity.

Accessories Burners, boiler controls, safety valves, gauges, fuel-oil-tank pumps, heater, and connections (strict code requirements). In certain areas, boilers must now comply with the regulations of a local (or national) air-resources commission. Boiler installations in general are subject to strict code requirements.

Noise, Vibration, and Heat Insulation

Vibration-isolation bases under all motor-driven equipment. Spring-supported isolation for fans and for all ceiling-mounted equipment. Inertial and spring isolation for refrigeration machines. Spring isolation for horizontal piping. Rubber-pad isolation under supports of vertical piping. Spring isolation of cooling towers. Duct-noise insulation as discussed under sheet-metal work, above.

Insulation should be covered in a general clause, e.g., "All piping, ductwork and equipment that transmits or receives heat or that will form condensation or is subject to freezing shall be insulated unless it is specifically stated otherwise." Some samples of proper insulation are given in Table 10-1.

Painting and Miscellaneous

Painting materials All exterior surfaces unless otherwise specifically omitted are to be prime-coated. Zinc chromate priming for all material exposed to weather. Lead and oil-paint primer for all machinery. Rust-O-leum for surfaces subject to constant moisture.

TABLE 10-1 SOME SAMPLES OF PROPER INSULATION

Equipment or condition	Insulation
Chilled water, up to and including 4 in	1-in fiber glass
5–10 in	1½-in fiber glass
Secondary water, through 2 in	1-in fiber glass
Steam, 0–15 lb/in², through 2 in	1½-in fiber glass
Over 2 in	2½-in fiber glass
Boiler feed lines	2-in fiber glass
Valves and pipe fittings	Same thickness as pipe
Fresh-air intake	1½-in fiber-glass board with vapor seal
Conditioned air supply and return, exposed	2-in fiber-glass board with vapor seal
Concealed	1½-in as above
Boiler and incinerator breechings and flues	4-in calcium silicate
Cold parts of refrigeration machines	2-in fiber glass with vapor seal
Kitchen-hood exhaust fans	2-in calcium silicate

Pipe identification   Use of painted or vinyl-cloth-colored code markers at valves, on either side of walls, and not more than 25 ft apart on horizontal runs or 5 ft above each floor on vertical runs.

Miscellaneous checklist   Thermometers, gauges, access doors, smoke indicators, automatic smoke detection, water and airflow metering, recording meters, alarm annunciators.

Water treatment   All chemicals used must comply with pollution controls. Chemicals used for control of scale, corrosion, microbiological growths, and pH. Condenser water pH to be between 6.5 and 7.0. Closed water-circulating systems pH to be between 7.5 and 9.0.

Temporary heat   To be written into specification or special conditions.

10-12 PLUMBING AND SPRINKLERS

General Note

For obvious reasons plumbing work is very carefully supervised by the building authorities. The code is very strict about how the work should be installed and tested and what materials can be used. The general note for Sec. 10-11 applies here as well.

Miscellaneous Work

If the plans for a recycling job call for plumbing lines to be laid below the existing basement grade, the plumbing contractor and the architect must be sure that the subgrade lines are laid in firm soil to avoid breakage or changes in grade by settlement. If there is any doubt, it is best to specify pipe saddles, which can be made part of the original bid specifications.

The architect or engineer should decide whether the plumbing or concrete contractor will build the bases for all pumps, heaters, and other apparatus. The plumber should also be made responsible for vibration and sound isolation of his work, access doors, pipe and valve identification, and necessary drip pans.

Temporary heat, light, and power takes in the plumbing, heating, and electrical contractors; the architect should specify exactly what he requires from all three.

Motors and controllers for plumbing equipment are normally furnished and installed by the electrical contractor, but there may be cases where the plumber will furnish the equipment to be connected by others. The architect should make it clear which contractor does what.

Materials and Piping

The kind of material used and the methods of installation are the same for a recycling as for new construction. In recycling the architect and engineer will try to salvage as much as they can of the existing installation. While this saves time and money, it also presents difficulties in connecting the new to the old. There is always the problem of using dissimilar metals because of possible electrolytic corrosion.

Material for piping can be cast iron or polyvinyl chloride (which is now allowed by many codes) for soil lines. It can be bell and spigot or no-hub. For water lines the piping can be ductile iron, cast iron, steel, brass, and copper type K or L (the K being used for underground work). The iron and steel can be galvanized. Lead pipe for sanitary drainage at water closets has been replaced to a large extent by special fittings which connect directly from the fixture to the waste line by means of bolted, gasketed connections. There is also a choice of vitrified tile pipe and asbestos-cement pipe for underground work. Many codes do not allow solder joints on copper tubing for water lines but do allow high-temperature brazed joints. This is a more expensive process and requires skilled workers. Victualic fittings, allowed in some codes, require less field work than screw or flanged joints. Valves on any one job should all be of the same manufacture.

The architect and engineer must not forget supports for vertical piping, proper hangers for horizontal piping, and provisions for expansion joints.

Sanitary Drainage and Storm Water

In a building to be recycled the sanitary and storm-water lines and the necessary disposal may already be in place. In older buildings the systems must usually be replaced or added to. If the occupancy of the building is to be changed to more intensive use, the system will probably have to be added to by ejector pits and pumps and/or sump pits and pumps, which come in many styles. A partly wet basement can sometimes be drained by a subsoil drainage system consisting of porous pipe laid in crushed stone leading to a drainage pit.

Hot-Water Heaters

Hot-water heaters are a combination of storage tank and heat exchanger. The tank can be a steel shell lined with cement, copper, copper silicon, or glass. It can be vertical or horizontal. The heat can be supplied by steam coils or electrically heated submersion units. All hot-water heaters should be heavily insulated (at least 1½ in of high-density glass fiber). All commercial or multifamily buildings should have hot-water circulating pumps.

Roof Tanks and Pumps

Codes call for buildings of certain sizes and heights to be protected by roof tanks, which in addition to supplying domestic water must have a certain fire reserve and be fed by water and fire pumps. Many old buildings have wooden roof tanks, which may or may not meet code requirements or which may be seriously deteriorated.

Fixtures

The architect has a choice of many styles and materials. The few basic specifications that should apply to all fixtures should include the following:

Faucets should be renewable-seat type and should have indices. They should be of brass, Monel, or stainless steel and be chrome-plated.

Each fixture should have its own turn-off valve.

All exposed supply and wastes should be chrome-plated.

Flush valves should be equipped with a vacuum-breaker device.

Chair carriers or other devices for supporting fixtures should be rigidly fastened to a secure wall or other support.

Insulation

All piping in exposed places must be frostproofed. Hot-water heaters come factory-insulated or should be covered with 2-in calcium silicate with wire mesh and hard-troweled finish. Chilled-drinking-water lines should be insulated with 1½-in premolded glass fiber. Hot- and cold-water lines should be covered with ½-in premolded glass fiber. All valves and fittings should be covered to the same thickness as the lines.

Sprinklers

Sprinklers should be new spray type with ½-in discharge orifice. The normal operating temperature for sprinklers is between 160 and 175°F. Sprinkler lines should be so installed that all or part of them can be drained. Sprinkler lines and standpipe lines must be connected to a siamese connection at an easily accessible point. Depending on location, sprinkler systems can be of the wet or dry type. The dry type requires the use of an air compressor. All sprinklers must be connected to a sprinkler alarm and a water-flow detector. Sprinkler systems are rigidly inspected by the local fire authorities.

Tests

Codes provide for testing fire lines, hot- and cold-water systems, and sanitary systems. Local officials have preferences as to how and when the tests are made. The specification should include preparation for, and making of, all tests by the subcontractor to the satisfaction of the proper authority and obtaining any necessary certificates of approval.

10-13 ELECTRICAL INSTALLATION

General

It is often possible in recycling to salvage and reuse portions of the electrical installation, especially if the existing building has been built within the past several decades, when electrical codes were in existence in almost their present form. With the newer intensive use the service will probably have to be reinforced, and more sophisticated controls will need to be installed, but some of the switch gear, circuit wiring, and other basic installations may be salvaged.

Because of the inherent danger of faulty installations electrical work is rigidly specified by code and rigidly inspected.

The specifications should call for prior approval of all materials and equipment, approval of shop drawings, and the contractor's responsibility for obtaining all necessary approvals and certificates.

Electric Service

The specification should state that the contractor must comply with all the rules and regulations of the power company, whether or not specifically mentioned. The contractor picks up the lines at the transformer station and is then responsible for the complete installation. This is especially true in recyclings where some of the electric system may be salvaged. Power company requirements may have changed since the original installation, and the entire installation, new and old, must comply.

Switchboards and Switch Gear

All electrical installations including switch gear, wiring, equipment, outlets, panel boards, etc., are governed by the rules and regulations of the National Electrical Code, National Electric Manufacturers Association (NEMA), Underwriters Laboratories, Inc. (ULI), and American National Standards Institute (ANSI). Other associations set standards of performance, but these are the basic ones.

Switchboards are free-standing, metal-enclosed with front access only. Switch gear is metal-enclosed with code-approved protective devices.

Conduits

Conduit for interior circuits is specified as aluminum except that branch wiring to fixtures or in metal or dry-wall partitions may be hot-dipped galvanized steel, aluminum, flexible metallic, or electrical metallic tubing. Exposed conduit in outdoor or damp locations indoors must be of aluminum with noncorrosive fittings. Conduit buried in concrete should be of steel. The architect should be particularly careful that conduit in reinforced concrete runs parallel to the main reinforcement. Conduit can also be of polyvinyl chloride, cement asbestos, or heavyweight fiber. In certain wet locations liquidtight conduit must be used.

Conductors

All control wiring is usually of no. 14 AWG, while wire for branch circuits is usually no. 12 AWG. Number 10 wire is to be used for more than three-wire circuits that supply fluorescents or high-intensity-discharge fixtures. Either aluminum or annealed copper may be used, but the wire gauge as shown above is for copper. Aluminum wiring is not recommended.

Lighting Fixtures

All lighting fixtures should carry an underwriters label. The specification should call for the contractor to lamp and/or relamp all fixtures. Fixtures enclosures should be a minimum of 20-gauge steel sheet or other metals equivalent in strength. The steel should receive a five-stage phosphate-base bonding material before painting. Lenses for fluorescent fixtures are usually specified as acrylic with a yellowness factor not to exceed 3 after 2000 h of exposure. Lenses for incandescent fixtures are usually specified of tempered glass.

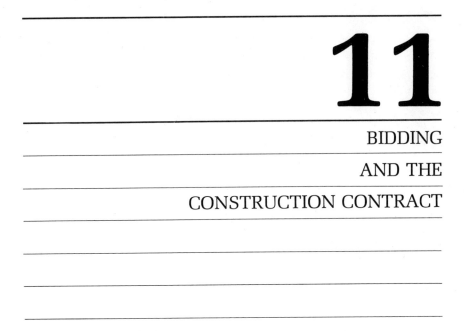

11

BIDDING

AND THE

CONSTRUCTION CONTRACT

11-1 THE BIDDING PROCEDURE

The bidding documents prepared for a recycling project should, if possible, be even more precise than those for a new building because a recycling job is more complicated. The plans and specifications, which spell out exactly what is to be done, what is to remain and what is to be new, reflect this fact.

For instance, every specification for a new building calls for the contractor to visit the site. The specification for a recycling should call for the bidder to inspect the existing building as well as the site, to satisfy himself that the work as shown in the plans and specifications can be completed within the set parameters. The bid proposal should make it clear that by signing the proposal the bidder has waived all rights to plead any misunderstanding as to quantities and conditions that may result in any future claims for extras.

Such a warning clause inserted in the request for bid alerts the bidder to examine existing conditions carefully and to bring his subcontractors to the site so that they can give him the benefit of their expertise in their particular trades. The developer and the architect should call all the bidders' attention to this clause. Misunderstandings and disputes *after* a construction job is started can be extremely expensive.

There is one other important caution. Extensive alteration work is a separate branch of construction, and not every builder knows how to bid it or how to go about performing the work in the most expeditious manner. The architect and owner should confine their bidders' list to contractors who are experienced in alteration work. It is well to qualify the bidders by investigating their financial capacity and previous experience. Even if no bond is required, a bidder who is able to obtain a bond is a fairly good risk. It is suggested that in complicated jobs the owner, architect, and contractor do not deal at arm's length but try for a meeting of the minds.

11-2   THE BIDDING DOCUMENTS

The bidding documents are used first in obtaining bids and then with the construction contract become the contract documents. There are several essential parts:

A complete list of the plans by number and date

The specifications

The general conditions of the Contract[1]

A complete list of the addenda to the plans and specifications

The proposal form, which the bidder must complete and sign[2]

11-3   EVALUATING THE BIDS

The bid request form always gives the owner and architect a period of time (usually about 30 days) for evaluating the bids. The first step is to examine each bid to see that it is responsive, i.e., that it answers every

---

[1]Many architects use AIA Document Form A201, which should not be modified without legal advice.

[2]Many architects use an AIA Document, but others use a proposal form tailored to the job. The proposal should contain requests for various alternates (if any) and for unit prices. Many proposals ask the bidder to break his bid down by trades such as the general construction and the electrical and mechanical trades. The proposal form should also give a specific day and hour for opening of bids. It should also state that the owner may refuse to accept any or all of the bids.

question and that it contains every figure that is called for. A nonresponsive bidder can be a careless bidder who may cause trouble later.

Even though the list of bidders may have been chosen with some care, now is the time to make doubly sure that the bidder or bidders who are being seriously considered are financially able to carry out the contract. In private construction it is ethical for the owner and architect to call in any or all bidders to discuss the scope of the job or the prices, so long as no competitive prices are revealed. This meeting can be extremely useful. It will tell the contractor what is expected of him and will reveal to the owner and architect how the contractor feels about his obligations, whether he is "extra happy" or whether he contemplates the job as a whole to be completed within his bid price and on time. Bidders should also be asked for time- and money-saving suggestions. In the writer's experience, bidders have often suggested changes which result in substantial savings, especially in the electrical and mechanical trades.

11-4   THE CONSTRUCTION CONTRACT

The Owner Acting as General Contractor

It is not advisable for the owner to act as his own general contractor unless he has extensive experience in general construction and in alteration work and has an organization in being. As an end result he may or may not save the general contractor's fee. Subcontractors are much more likely to give their best price to a general contractor who is constantly doing business, in the hope that they may get return business. For the same reason they are not so apt to claim extras for the smaller changes or for job conditions that no construction job can ever avoid.

The General Provisions of Any Construction Contract

Every contract must contain certain basic information to make it valid. The following items may sound rudimentary, but it is surprising how many times some of them are forgotten.

The legal name and address of the owner

The name and address of the contractor

The date of the contract

The location of the work

The description of the work

The proposed starting and completion dates

A general note stating what the contractor is to furnish, such as material, equipment, labor, insurance, job protection, etc.

The price for the work, including accepted alternates and unit prices (the owner should make sure that no provision for escalation is expressed or implied unless it is as a result of deliberate negotiations)

How payments are to be made

Other provisions regarding such matters as default, arbitration procedures, assignments or termination of the contract, changes in the work, etc.

Types of Contracts

All construction contracts contain the same basic provisions. They vary only in the methods of pricing and in the manner and conditions under which payments are to be made.

THE LUMP-SUM OR STIPULATED-SUM CONTRACT

It is advantageous for the owner to obtain a construction contract which holds the contractor to a stipulated sum. Such a contract can enable the owner to go ahead with his financial planning with some assurance. But the contract which holds the contractor to a fixed price also imposes some very definite obligations on the owner and the architect. While most contractors do not deliberately look for extras, a great many have become quite sophisticated about their obligations and their rights under a contract. This calls for special care on the part of the owner and the architect, who must make sure that every item of the construction is mentioned in the specifications or is shown on the drawings. Catch-all phrases which are added to the description of a piece of work such as "and all work incidental to the work specified in the plans and specifications" are no longer held valid in contract disputes.

This specificity is very important in a recycling project, where some parts of the work call for demolition, some call for repair or replacement, and some call for entirely new work.

There have been many successfully completed recycling projects under the stipulated-sum contract, although there are bound to be job conditions that call for added payments to the contractor. The owner must therefore set aside a contingency fund for such extras. A usual amount is 5 percent of the contract amount; less is dangerous. In one case the contingency fund was too small to pay for all the unforeseen conditions that arose. No extra money was available. The architect had to cut down on some work that was desirable but not essential and on some quality in order to balance his budget.

THE COST-PLUS-FIXED OR PERCENTAGE-FEE CONTRACT

This type of contract is not recommended. The contractor has no real incentive to keep costs down. Even if the contractor presents a budget figure, he is under no obligation to keep to it, and this type of contract is notorious for cost overruns. It is much better for the owner and architect to spend additional time and expense to investigate thoroughly and define the work specifically than to rely on the tender mercies of a contractor. He may be completely honest, but his workmen and his subcontractors will certainly know that this is a cost-plus job, and the temptation is great. The only possible way to control a cost-plus job, if it must be so, is to carefully define what items the contractor can include in his cost. It should state clearly that the contractor must use his best efforts to protect the owner by incurring only those costs which are necessary for the proper performance of the work.

THE GUARANTEED-MAXIMUM-PLUS-FIXED-FEE CONTRACT

The cost-plus contract can be modified so that both the owner and the contractor are protected by requiring the contractor to set a maximum price on the contract and to state the amount of his fee. In usual practice the maximum price in such a contract is higher than it might be in a stipulated sum, but most of such contracts also contain a saving clause, which guarantees to the contractor a percentage of all he saves under the stated maximum. This contract assures the owner of the maximum price he will have to pay. Under such a contract the owner should have the right to audit the contractor's books to be sure that only costs applicable to the work are charged.

THE NEGOTIATED CONTRACT

If the entrepreneur and/or the architect have particularly close relations with a general contractor or with a mechanical or electrical contractor, it is possible that all or part of the construction contract can be negotiated. This can be the case when the plans and specifications have not been fully developed but there is need for quick completion. Even then and with the best of good faith on both sides, it is well to define the parameters of the work clearly. One other caution: it is not at all certain that a negotiated contract produces the lowest cost, but this can be considered a trade-off for accelerated construction.

11-5 THE OWNER'S OBLIGATIONS

A construction contract is an agreement between the owner and the contractor which defines among other things the duties and obligations of each party. The first obligation of the owner is to provide the architect with sufficient information (see Chap. 7) to plan the work properly. The owner should also be sure that his requirements are clearly settled and clearly stated before the work is awarded. Changes in scope during the course of a construction job can be costly and may cause serious delay. The courts have held that contractors are entitled to be reimbursed for delays caused by the owner.

11-6 CHANGES DURING CONSTRUCTION

Even with the best intentions on everyone's part, changes in the work during construction are almost inevitable. That is why every contract should carry a change clause which provides for an orderly method for proposing changes in the work, for arriving at just compensation, and for payment. This is especially important in a recycling job. There are many reasons for changes, and it may be helpful to the owner, the developer, etc., to list them here.

Change due to Advanced Technology

Materials and methods of construction are in constant change, and it is possible that a new method of insulation, a new type of lighting fixture, a major improvement in air-conditioning equipment or fenestration, etc., may be put on the market before the job has reached that stage. This can be very tricky if the specified material is on firm order, but if the new process or material is important enough, a trade-off may be possible.

Change due to Additional Work

Sometimes an owner or architect may be able to cover such work by asking the contractor for an alternate price to cover it. The contractor will protect himself by giving the owner a certain amount of time to accept or reject this alternate. If it is accepted, no other change order is necessary. But in many cases the additional work may be caused by the requirements of a tenant for such things as extra floor loading for filing or a library or double fenestration and extra air conditioning for a computer. In such instances the owner and architect are obliged to issue an immediate stop order in writing on the work going on at these points or face the expense of tearing out as well as rebuilding.

Changes Caused by Errors in Planning

It is possible for the architect or engineer to misstate a dimension so that more than one piece of construction is shown in the same place, or he may omit a ladder or a piece of railing or a small piece of equipment. This can often become the basis for a disagreement. The architect's contention is that the chiller unit cannot work without a pump or that one needs a fixed rail on an iron stair whether it is shown or not. The contractor's contention is always that he did not price it because it was not on the plan. Why didn't he or his subcontractor call attention to the omission when they were estimating the job? In many cases the dispute is resolved by splitting the cost down the middle.

Changes Caused by Noncompliance with Code

Many times the regulatory authorities have refused to grant a certificate of occupancy or have issued a stop order during the progress of the work because of noncompliance with the building code. Architects' specifications always state that the contractor must comply with all codes and all governmental authorities having jurisdiction. This clause is to some extent a catch-all, which places the burden of compliance on the contractor. In recycling work it is likely that the original structure was built before the present code was in force, and many mechanical and structural portions of the building are therefore noncomplying. The burden of compliance rests to a large extent on the architect, who must be completely familiar with the code.

But the contractor and his subcontractors must also be familiar with the code. A typical specification clause will state "The Contractor shall . . . comply with all laws, ordinances, rules, regulations of any public authority. . . . If the contractor observes that any of the contract documents are at variance . . . , he shall promptly notify the Architect in writing. . . ." In cases where the contractor has not notified the architect or has not followed the specifications, he is not entitled to any increase in the contract price caused by the extra work necessary to comply.

There are borderline cases, e.g., one in which a contractor was given to understand by the plans that it was all right to combine a storm and sanitary sewer and by some error the plans that showed this were passed by the local building department. A building inspector stopped the job because this is a violation of the plumbing code (as it always is). The plumbing contractor who had done work in the community should have been aware of this, but he never questioned it. The extra cost had to be shared by the owner and the contractor.

Changes Caused by Site Conditions

The best way to handle this situation is to call for unit prices to cover any unforeseen conditions. Such units protect the owner from future exorbitant charges for price and quantity. Under such a provision in the contract the contractor must immediately call the architect's attention to any work which he considers beyond the scope of his contract, and this gives the architect an opportunity to measure the quantities of the work in question. In recycling, such items of work can consist of new footings or a deeper basement which may involve rock or water, unseen deteriorated masonry or timbers, deteriorated piping which may not show, etc.

Changes or Extra Charges Caused by Delay

Some delays in construction are excusable, and some are not. For instance, a delay caused by a labor dispute on the site or at a factory supplying essential material or a delay by authority in granting certain permits is excusable. On the other hand, a delay caused by an owner's not being able to make up his mind or an owner's financial difficulties can result in a contractor's claim for damages. In any construction job, whether new or recycling, many materials and essential pieces of equipment must be ordered well in advance. Inability on the owner's or architect's part to make a choice can lead to a claim for delay.

11-7 COMPENSATION

Any construction contract must specify the amount, the method and the time when the contractor is to be paid. The amount consists of the total of all the work done up to a specified time less the retention which must be clearly stated. The AIA Form (Stipulated Sum Contract) under "progress payments" gives the wording which is generally followed in all contracts. The owner and architect must set up the necessary procedures with the construction lender so that payment can be made upon receipt of the architect's certification of the request for payment. The architect and the owner's and the lender's representatives (if there are any) must be sure to inspect the work as soon as the request for payment is received.

The contractor must provide backup material showing the percentage of completion of each piece of the work against his original breakdown of the cost of the work by trades. The owner or architect should be sure, right at the start, that the breakdown is not forward-loaded to provide a disproportionate amount of payment to the contractor at the early stages of the job.

It is important that a general contractor be paid fairly and promptly and that he treat his subcontractors in a like manner. Such payment leads to good work done on time and with less temptation to skimp on the details.

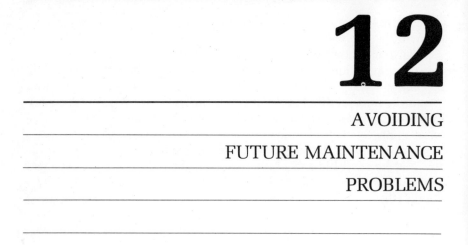

12

AVOIDING
FUTURE MAINTENANCE
PROBLEMS

12-1 SPECIAL CONSIDERATIONS IN RECYCLING

From the very inception of a recycling project the architect and the owner should be aware that what they now build will have to be maintained during the life of the building. The ease and expense of maintenance is a very important factor in the profitability and rentability of a building. Tenants subject to roof leaks, plumbing leaks, or breakdowns of heating or cooling are not happy tenants.

A recycling project is a combination of existing and new structural and mechanical systems. It is important that it be done as economically as possible. But sometimes an immediate saving that can be made by leaving a piece of doubtful old work in place can cause a future serious maintenance problem in an inaccessible place. It is a matter of informed judgment.

12-2 INSPECTION DURING CONSTRUCTION

The architect should make a list of inspection priorities. As buildings are built for protection from the weather, one of the first priorities is to keep weather out of the building. This means careful inspection of roofing, flashing, exterior wall structure, window openings, caulking, and any exterior structures subject to weather such as entrance porticos, penthouses, skylights, elevator bulkheads, and so on. All these pieces of work cannot be looked at constantly as they are being built, but there are certain times when they should be inspected. For instance, once the architect is satisfied that the roofer is using the proper amount of pitch and the proper weight of roofing felt and is overlapping properly, he can turn his attention to other matters, but he must watch carefully to see that the flashing is properly soldered and is overlapped by the specified amount by the roofing. He must see to it that expansion joints are placed where they are shown in the plan. The caulking of all joints in the exterior skin must be constantly spot-checked. If the exterior wall is of masonry, the inspector must see to it that all the new work is fully bedded in mortar and that the back of the masonry is fully slushed with mortar. The glazing is very important. A vulnerable spot for water leakage is between glass and frame. Any neoprene gasketing which keeps the glass from contact with a metal frame must be checked. This can prevent water leakage as well as the possible cracking of the glass.

Another cause of trouble is noise. The specifications may be explicit about all the precautions the contractor must take to avoid sound transmission by air leakage or by vibration. In spite of this, a careless workman can undo the most carefully laid plans by allowing a water line to lie directly on a steel beam and transmit the pump vibration to the steel structure or by forgetting a sound-attenuator lining in a duct. If the sound barrier between two offices sharing a perimeter air-conditioning enclosure is left out, one salesman can listen to another salesman's conversations. Not all these troubles can be eliminated, but inspection of sensitive areas can stop some of them.

Cracks in walls and ceilings are a cause of annoyance. The architect must make sure that expansion joints are properly installed and that walls are properly anchored and ceilings securely hung.

Because recycling is a combination of the new and the old, the architect must be specially alert about the attachment of new plumbing, heating, or electrical lines to existing work. The specification can be exact about removing existing work back to a certain point, but if a contractor uncovers mechanical lines that seem to look good, he may not remove them. Air ducts that seem in good condition may not be lined properly for sound attenuation. There may be mechanical lines that will become very difficult of access when the new work is completed. All existing work left in place can present a future maintenance problem.

Old structural work must also be inspected carefully to be sure that it can support any new loads to be placed on it and that the new work will support it with sufficient bearing. The new work, of course, must bear on firm support.

12-3 MAINTENANCE CONSIDERATIONS IN SPECIFYING MATERIALS

For the architect to specify the very best obtainable material and appliances for a project is a fairly sure but expensive way to reduce future maintenance, but there are many materials that are almost as good as the very best and considerably less expensive. This can range from structural lumber and cabinet work to toilet accessories and mechanical and electrical devices. A study of structural, electrical, and plumbing codes will be rewarding, as will be a request for suggestions from contractors. The author in his experience has found many materials and devices which are able to perform efficiently, which are trouble-free over a long period of time, and which can be considerably less expensive than some of their highly touted competitors.

12-4 FORWARD PLANNING

Forward planning in the design can avert many later problems, some of which are very costly to correct after the building is completed. A simple example is providing a large enough electric service for unforeseen future needs. Some lack of forethought can be ludicrous, as in the case of the boiler that needed retubing. It was so close to a masonry wall that the tubes could not be pulled out or new ones put in. The wall had to be practically torn down.

Forward planning will allow for extra electric service in a large building by specifying an empty conduit to be run up through a pipe shaft, or the use of a bus duct with spare capacity, or allowing plenty of extra room in underfloor electric ducts. It may call for the plumbing contractor to install empty wastes, vents, and water lines in one or more locations in an office building to allow for future toilet rooms or other use of plumbing facilities.

Sometimes there may be a requirement over and above the normal. Perhaps an occupying tenant, with whom negotiations are going on while the building is under construction, has a special requirement for large catalog mailings or has very heavy interfloor traffic in people or papers. In such a case an alert owner or architect-engineer can probably arrange for a heavy-duty dumbwaiter or even an extra elevator (if there is time) and can probably get the tenant to pay for at least part of it.

Requirements for special sound insulation should be designed for, and built into, a building if the foreseeable future occupancy is likely to call for it. Many architect-engineers design extra-heavy steel for certain portions of the floor areas to accommodate future requirements for heavy floor loading by computers, files, or other special tenant equipment.

The final purpose of the building will to a great extent serve to determine the amount of forward planning necessary. It will also help to determine the kinds and qualities of materials to be used.

12-5   SCHEDULING MAINTENANCE

Section 12-3 has mentioned that the choice of good quality equipment and material can help a great deal toward the avoidance of future maintenance problems. But to install good materials and not to maintain them is poor management. Benign neglect does not work here.

It is recommended, especially in the case of a recycling, that the owner (or manager), the architect, and the engineer get together some time toward the end of the construction to put together a schedule of maintenance which will identify the pieces of equipment or construction, how often they are to be inspected, how often they are to be lubricated, cleaned, or replaced, and who is to be responsible.

Table 12-1 gives only a very small sampling. Proper maintenance is a profitable exercise in management.

TABLE 12-1   TYPICAL ITEMS ON A MAINTENANCE SCHEDULE

Item	Frequency of inspection	Action to be taken
Evaporative condenser	Once a month	Check for leaks in joints, dirt on coil surfaces, dirt or obstructions on air-inlet screen, pump-screen spray nozzle, or water distribution holes; check pH of water
Lighting efficiency	Every 3 months	Wipe lamps clean; when light output of a group of lamps falls below 70% of original, relamp entire group
Caulking	Annually	Look for cracks, loose caulking, dried-out caulking cracks in masonry; note especially condition of caulking around large openings

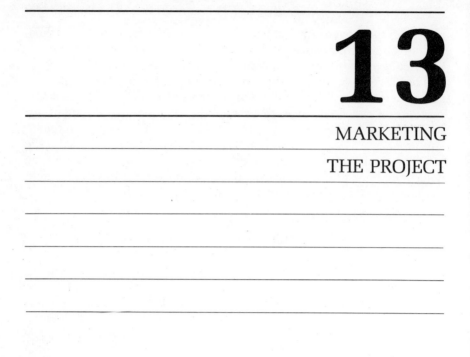

13

MARKETING

THE PROJECT

13-1 THE IMPORTANCE OF MARKETING IN RECYCLING

One of the important questions an entrepreneur or architect must ask is how well the completed project will sell or rent. Several previous chapters have been devoted to determining the right location, the right building, and the particular use for the project which will have the most appeal in the rental market. These determinations are the same whatever the final use of the recycled building is to be. It may be a computer center or a factory in a somewhat rundown neighborhood or an apartment building or office building in an older mixed business-residential area, but the basic question the developer must ask is: Will it rent and/or eventually sell?

13-2 THE PRINCIPLES OF MARKETING REAL ESTATE

The product that is for sale or rent determines how and by what means it is to be marketed. There are a number of fundamental principles in

112

any marketing effort. The following refer specifically to the renting or sales of real estate.

How to Motivate the Consumer

Show that this product will satisfy a need, latent or real. There are many people who would like to live or work in "different" neighborhoods.

Emphasize nearness to work or to home, proximity to shopping, good transportation, proximity to the business center, or to the amenities required by householders.

Show that this project will appeal to individuality; that its architecture or location can be a "conversation piece," and that living or working here will confer some prestige.

Emphasize the competitive rental rates or in the case of condominiums the competitive sales price. Mention again what the tenant or purchaser is getting for his rent or sales dollar.

Emphasize that recycling and living or working in a recycled building are becoming fashionable. The tenant is helping save material and energy. This may act as an added incentive to many people.

How to Reach the Consumer

The means of communication with the prospective tenant is determined by which real estate product is being sold.

RESIDENTIAL PROJECTS

The following steps are suggested for a residential project.

1. Advertising in local newspapers with emphasis on the fact that this is a recycled project with special architectural or neighborhood appeal (or both). *The advertisement must be worded to appeal to the kind of people who are attracted by unconformity.*

2. Printed flyers to selected prospects. A telephone book giving tenants by address can be obtained in some localities. *Personally* addressed letters to the tenants of selected residential buildings have proved useful. This form of advertising can be used for condominiums as well.

3.   Advertising signs are not used as much as they should be. Certainly an attractive sign on the property is useful to tell the passing public what is being done. Such a sign should also tell where to call or write for further information.

4.   Articles in the real estate pages of the local newspaper will serve to bring attention to the project. Newspapers are always willing to print a story with a different angle.

5.   The owner should try to obtain permission from nearby offices to post a notice on the bulletin board.

6.   Many large companies maintain housing relocation offices for their transferred personnel. If the project is located near a headquarters office or a regional office, it would be worthwhile to advise the company's relocation service that this housing is available.

7.   Real estate management and brokerage firms are available in all large communities and in many smaller ones. The owner should choose a firm that employs only full-time professionals. This of course entails rental commissions and possible management commissions if the service is continued.

OFFICE BUILDINGS

Marketing an office building must be directed toward the businessman. It must show that renting in this project is advantageous to his business. The appeal can be made by means of lower rentals, which means lower overhead; the uniqueness of the project and location, which may mean that the tenant is not lost in the maze of a huge office building; the proximity (if this is so) of the office to residential areas (the ability to walk to work is a persuasive argument, especially in these days of chaotic mass transportation); and finally the fact that the businessman can take advantage of doing business in this location by specifically advising his clients or customers or prospective employees of his new unique location. The foregoing sales points can be communicated by several means.

As newspapers are a means of mass communication, it is necessary in the case of a recycled office building to appeal to a small special clientele. This must be done by an advertisement that will catch this special attention.

The owner may wish to appeal to a certain type of prospect such as a law office, a smaller advertising agency, an architect, or an insurance firm. If so, he can direct his advertising toward such people and indicate the advantages of this special building or location to their business.

A good brochure can be expensive, but it also attracts tenants. Its distribution must be strictly limited to the special people who would be interested in a project of this type.

Many real estate brokerage firms specialize in office rentals. The owner should employ one of these firms. The good ones have wide contacts and cross listings with other firms. If a firm gets an exclusive, it should help with the advertising cost.

SPECIALTY BUILDINGS

A specialized use may be as a computer center, a neighborhood medical building, a light-manufacturing or assembly center, a branch office of a downtown office to be used for mass filing and archives.

The question may arise why an architect or entrepreneur would want to recycle a building for a specialized purpose with limited marketing appeal. The answer is that the entrepreneur does not enter such a recycling project without strong indications that it will be rented. The indication may be letters of intent from medical people, business firms, or a computer company stating their need and readiness to furnish and use a centralized computer or any other firm indications of this kind.

These firm offers to rent must be solicited by the entrepreneur who sees a building which lends itself to a particular purpose and who then must sell the idea of the use of the building to the particular business involved. If a medical building is near a downtown business center, he can emphasize lower rents, the proximity of present or future patients who work full time, and the special style or other unique features of the building which differ from a downtown office building. The structure may be a partly used warehouse or a former manufacturing building which is structurally sound for heavy floor loading and which can be recycled for computers or heavy filing or, depending on the neighborhood, for light manufacturing or assembly. In every one of these cases rental offers must be solicited before the recycling goes ahead. Each offer must point out the special advantages.

It is not necessary to have the building fully rented before work starts, but there must be firm evidence that the guaranteed rental income will at least cover all fixed charges including taxes, mortgage interest, and amortization.

13-3   PRIOR MAJOR COMMITMENT

If the developer is fortunate enough to obtain a major commitment from a financially responsible prospect to recycle a building for a specific purpose, he can start immediately after negotiations are complete. The architect or developer can take the position of a part owner or simply participate as a professional who is paid a fee. If the recycler takes an ownership position, he must be sure that the commitment and subsequent lease are for a period long enough to give him flexibility in rerenting the structure. He must also be sure that the recycling is designed so that the building can be changed to another use without major expense. If the major commitment is for a large amount of space but not for all available space, the entrepreneur should make every effort to rent space for related uses if possible, creating a mutually beneficial relationship between tenants which can be very good for the occupancy rate.

MANAGEMENT

OF THE

COMPLETED PROJECT

14-1 ESSENTIALS OF BUILDING MANAGEMENT

The objective of successful building management should be obvious, but it bears repeating. It is to maintain the income and the physical condition of the property to the fullest possible extent. Management starts with marketing the project, selling or leasing space at the highest possible price (which is set by market conditions), and preserving the physical condition of the property at the best possible level consistent with cost.

14-2 OWNER VS. PROFESSIONAL RENTING

Whether the owner should manage a recycled building depends on a variety of circumstances, the principal ones being the profession, knowledge, and expertise of the owner or entrepreneur and the nature of the final product. Many recyclings are originated by architects who carry through the entire project from finding the property and the working drawings to the completion of construction and the subsequent renting.

The Owner as Rental Agent

The rental effort should begin when the project reaches the stage at which the architect and the entrepreneur have decided what the completed project will look like, how it will be divided for rental purposes, and what the rental rates will be. At this time the owner's first management attempt occurs. He now has to market the project and negotiate leases.

In rental housing or condominiums it is quite possible that proper advertising and a single rental agent employed on a temporary payroll or commission basis will accomplish the purpose. There will also be certain lease negotiations. This presupposes that the owner has sufficient time and knowledge of this extremely important subject. If he has not, the services of a professional may be indicated. Most rental brokers are also building management agents, and it is very easy to drift from the rental to the management stage.

The owner must then be prepared to pay not only the first rental commissions and the subsequent renewal rental commissions but also a percentage of the current gross rent roll (usually 5 percent) as a management fee. All these commissions can amount to a very substantial sum, which comes off the top of the income.

What is the alternative? The nature and complications of the property to be managed must determine this. An example of this can be found in some of the case studies that follow in Chaps. 17 to 20. In one case the end result of the recycling was a combination of residential condominiums, office space, and stores and restaurants. The architect was the principal. He not only found the property but was also the architect, the developer, and the majority owner.

The condominiums were sold by an individual sales agent who was employed on a temporary salary and commission basis. This person had previous experience in brokerage and real estate sales and was armed with brochures, condominium layouts, and sales prices. The marketing was pointed toward a specific group of people who would be interested in living in a historic waterfront location. All the condominiums were sold by the time the project was completed.

The Professional Broker

The rental of the offices, stores, and restaurants was also attempted by the owner, who employed a manager to rent and manage the project. However, the amount of space to be rented was so extensive that the job was finally given to a professional broker, who had the advantage of cross listings, which individuals do not have, and of knowing the going rental rates, the status of occupancy of other office buildings, and the date of expiration of the leases of prospective tenants. The broker also took charge of the advertising and promotion of all the commercial space. The good professional broker earns his commission, and unless an owner has had extensive experience, he is well advised to use a broker on any but the smallest projects.

How a Decision Can Be Made

At the start of the project one of the decisions that should be made is how the recycled structure can be most successfully rented.

RESIDENTIAL

Residential property can be rental property or a condominium. A small residential rental property can be rented by the owner just as easily as by a broker and with a consequent saving of commissions. A sample apartment, finished before the full completion, is of great help. A sign at the entrance with a safe walkway to the sample apartment will attract prospective tenants. A part-time agent without prior experience can be on the premises, especially on weekends. The lease itself can be negotiated by the owner. The same is true for condominiums. Some basic advertising, an agent on the premises, and a sample unit or even a good set of floor plans can be successful, and the consequent saving of sales commissions is very appreciable. It therefore seems that the owner can successfully rent or sell his own rental property or small condominium.

COMMERCIAL

Office space and street-floor store space are difficult to rent by an owner without real estate contacts. He can perform all the functions as set forth in Chap. 13 (Marketing) and try to rent as much as he can without the use of a rental broker, but the owner should set a time limit on his own efforts, say 6 months before the completion date. At that time, if the project has not been firmly leased to the point where the rentals will cover at least mortgage interest and taxes, consideration should be given to employing a rental broker who is experienced in commercial space.

This would also be true for computer space or space to be used for ancillary purposes by a business firm.

SPECIAL-PURPOSE BUILDINGS

A building should not be recycled for a specific purpose unless there is a strong indication that it can be rented for that purpose. Exceptions might be a small medical building near a hospital or close to a business center or a small building near the courthouse that would appeal to lawyers. In such cases the owner could attempt to rent them by appealing directly to these special groups and then use the same time limit set above. It is suggested that the owner use a part-time temporary agent who can at least ring doorbells, leave brochures, and speak to the nurse or receptionist if he cannot speak to a principal.

14-3 LEASES

The Essentials of a Lease

The lease for space is a very important document, and it is well for the owner to know the essential components of a lease. Printed lease forms are obtainable from the local real estate board or from a stationer. Lease forms vary in different states in order to comply with the local law, but every lease must contain the following information:

> The names of the lessor and the lessee
>
> An agreement between them to let the premises (the lessor, or landlord) and to take the premises (the lessee, or tenant)
>
> A description of the premises by a dimensioned drawing or other specific means
>
> The consideration, or the amount of rental to be paid, and a description as to how and when it is to be paid

Most state laws call for a written lease for a period of 1 year or more.

SERVICES BY OWNER

When the owner is setting the final rental rate, he must determine what services he will include in the rent, and the lease must state what services will be provided, e.g., cleaning, hot and cold water, heating, air conditioning, electricity, minor repairs, and other services.[1] For

---

[1] It is suggested that paragraph (b) of the typical lease be used.

heating and air conditioning the lease should define the parameters such as 68 or 70°F at 0°F outside. For air conditioning a differential should not exceed 15° between interior and exterior temperatures at 50 percent humidity. Electricity should be defined to be used only for normal office machines for commercial buildings. In residential buildings it is better to meter the tenants individually.

Following is a typical lease clause which defines an owner's services to a tenant.

The Landlord shall provide at the Landlord's expense except as otherwise provided

(a) Janitor service in and about the office space, Saturdays, Sundays, and holidays excepted

(b) Heat and, except for basement space, air conditioning, daily from 8 A.M. to 5 P.M., Saturdays, Sundays, and holidays excepted, sufficient to maintain comfortable temperature and humidity on the basis of one person per 100 ft² of space reasonably subdivided

(c) Hot and cold water for drinking, lavatory, and toilet purposes

(d) Passenger-elevator service at all times. Freight-elevator service daily from 8 A.M. to 5 P.M., Saturdays, Sundays, and holidays excepted; any or all elevator service may be automatic

(e) Window washing of all exterior windows, both inside and out, weather permitting

(f) Painting of interior during regular business hours, as required, but not more frequently than every 5 years, commencing 5 years after the commencement of the term hereof

(g) Reasonable amounts of electricity for ordinary lighting and the usual small business-machine purposes; providing, however, if Tenant uses IBM equipment or other large office machines on the Premises requiring additional electricity, such additional electricity shall be paid for by the Tenant

Any additional work or service of the character described above and any unusual amount of such work or service, including service furnished outside the stipulated hours, required by the Tenant shall be paid for by the Tenant at cost, plus 15 percent thereof for the Landlord's overhead. The Landlord does not warrant that any of the services above mentioned will be free from interruptions caused by repairs, renewals, improvements, alterations, strikes, lockouts, accidents, inability of the Landlord to obtain fuel or supplies, or other causes beyond the reasonable control of the Landlord. Any such interruption of service shall never be deemed an eviction or disturbance of the Tenant's use and possession of the Premises or any part thereof, or render the Landlord liable to the Tenant for damages, or relieve the Tenant from performance of the Tenant's obligation under this lease.

PERCENTAGE LEASES

Percentage leases are very prevalent for store rentals. The rule of thumb is to start with a minimum guaranteed rental of 60 to 70 percent of the fair rent and to then add a percentage of gross sales over the minimum. For instance if the fair rent of a store is $6000 per year, the minimum guarantee might be 60 percent of $6000 or $3600. If the percentage[1] rental for this type of business is 5 percent, the lease will state that the minimum rental will be in force up to the point when the sales amount to $72,000 per year. ($72,000 × 5% = $3600) The tenant must pay an extra amount to equal 5 percent of all sales over $72,000. At sales of $120,000 the rent would be $6000.

The owner is cautioned that percentage leases are not to be undertaken lightly and only with a responsible tenant who keeps only *one* set of books which can be audited.

ESCALATION

Every commercial lease should contain an escalation clause which enables the owner after a fixed base year to increase the total rent roll of the building by an amount equal to the increased cost of taxes, fuel, utilities, wages of building help, and general materials. There are many clauses which can be used. The local real estate board can recommend a standard form. The escalation clause is not usually inserted in a residential lease, with the result that the rent cannot be increased during the term of the lease. Many owners now grant only year-to-year leases so that the rent can be increased each year to meet rising costs.

NET LEASES

When a structure is recycled for a single tenant, or when a single tenant happens to occupy an entire building, an owner who does not want to be bothered with day-to-day management may enter into a net lease with the tenant. In such an instance the tenant pays a base rent to the owner and in addition pays for his own cleaning, heating, electricity, insurance, etc., and all taxes. There is also a net-net lease in which the

[1]Percentages vary for different business enterprises. The local real estate board will know.

tenant also pays the mortgage interest and amortization. This type of lease can only be made with a responsible tenant. In the case of the net lease the base rent should pay the owner enough to cover the mortgage interest and amortization plus a suitable return on his money equity and the money value of his time and effort in the planning and promotion of the project.

An experienced real estate attorney should be consulted in all lease matters.

14-4   HOW TO ORGANIZE THE MANAGEMENT

The architect or entrepreneur who wishes to manage his own recycled building must start by making a list of all the essential duties to be performed, so that he can gain the maximum possible return. But even before he starts, he should decide whether the time he will have to spend is worth the management fee he would have to pay a professional. Another consideration is that owner management can be financially rewarding because management companies cannot have the personal interest in tight control that an owner has.

What Must Be Done

A separate space must be provided for the management office. It can be a table, a filing cabinet and a telephone with its own number. Stationery (rent bills, letterheads, lease forms, order forms, payroll forms, etc.) and a set of bound ledgers should be provided. (An accountant should be consulted.)

A separate bank account should be provided under the management name.

The everyday duties of management must be delegated. It may be possible to add these duties to the workload of existing office help. An office bookkeeper would be most helpful. Some of these duties are:

Preparation and presentation of rent bills

Collection of rents and bank deposits

Follow-up of delinquent accounts

Payrolls

Ordering supplies, inventory control

Paying bills for materials, contracts, utilities, etc.

Payment of mortgage interest, taxes, insurance

Keeping a day-to-day tickler file (in a small project all these duties need not take more than a few hours a week)

Record keeping (the procedure should be set up by an accountant; The record keeping must keep the owner aware of his current financial position and serve for tax purposes)

14-5 SETTING UP A MAINTENANCE PROGRAM

The architect should be consulted by the owner and should be concerned with setting up a proper maintenance program. If the materials and methods of construction shown in his plans and described in his specifications have been properly used and the construction inspection properly carried out, there remains the matter of keeping everything well preserved and running smoothly.

Maintenance programs should be carefully thought through. Maintenance must be tailored to a building's size and the intended uses for its equipment. A small building with only a few men may have an entirely different program from a large building that can afford an expert in electrical maintenance, or boiler-room equipment, or plumbing. Manufacturers' recommendations should be studied and the interaction of equipment looked into to determine whether the failure of a small inexpensive part could cause a chain reaction and great damage. It is sometimes better to spend more on maintenance of certain equipment than seems economical in order to avoid tenant annoyance.

Sample Maintenance Procedure

The size and occupancy of the building and the lease provisions set the extent of the services to be rendered.

Cleaning of office buildings can be performed by a contractor or by the owner if only a few people are involved. In residential buildings a part-time or full-time janitor can perform this work.

Window washing, floor stripping and waxing should be given to a contractor (office building only).

Exterminating should be given to a contractor.

Elevator maintenance should be given to the elevator company.

Electrical, plumbing, and miscellaneous repairs can be made by a part-time handyman janitor.

Heating- and cooling-plant maintenance in a small office building can be done by a part-time handyman. There should be a schedule to tell when moving parts are to be oiled and cleaned.

Painting should be given to a contractor. Painting is done only as called for by the lease.

Supplies such as cleaning materials, electrical and plumbing devices, lamps, and toilet-room material can be purchased in small quantities for a small building and kept in a secure place with very few keys available.

14-6   LEGAL CONSIDERATIONS IN BUILDING MANAGEMENT

The owner of a recycled project will certainly obtain legal advice, but it is well for him to be acquainted with a few of the important legal considerations.

The first important one is the certificate of occupancy. Some communities issue a temporary as well as a permanent certificate. There is a difference between these certificates in the legal rights and obligations of an owner, which the owner should be aware of. The encroachment of one property on another can be serious. The usual law states that an encroachment lasting 10 years or over gives the encroaching party a legal right to the property by *adverse possession*.

Some of the laws relating to leases are:

Length of lease.   Any lease for a period of 1 year or more must be in writing.

Holdover clause.   Some leases still contain such a clause which calls for automatic renewal of the lease unless certain legal notice is given by either party. With rising costs this clause is not used very often, and the courts have been unsympathetic, especially in the case of residential tenants.

Constructive eviction.   A tenant can claim constructive eviction if the owner fails to furnish heat or hot water or allows the roof to leak or fails to repair any essential parts of the structure. Constructive eviction can generally be claimed when the landlord fails to provide a service called for by the lease.

Right to enter.   The landlord has the right to enter leased premises to make necessary repairs or, at a designated time before a lease expires, to show the premises to a prospective tenant.

General.   In general the written terms of the lease set forth the obligations of each party. The lease form should be approved by an attorney.

14-7   HOW TO DETERMINE RENTAL RATES

Comparison with Existing Rates

Chapter 5 discussed how to make a survey of existing, competitive rentals. There is a wide difference in rental rates, which depend on the neighborhood, the type of accommodation, the age of the building, the services rendered, etc. The owner of the recycled project must be sure that he is comparing like to like. The new high-rise downtown office building in a 100 percent location or the new apartment building in a strictly zoned residential area should charge the highest rents. But there are marginal older buildings on the periphery of the top areas which still charge fairly high rents and which can be considered competitive. The recycled project can charge rentals that may be slightly under these or equal to them if the project can offer certain advantages, e.g., architectural charm and convenience to transportation and amenities. The owner can then use these rental rates as a guide in setting his own rates.

The Financial Considerations

The primary considerations are to set the rental rate high enough to earn a reasonable return on the owner's equity money and low enough to attract tenants by its competitive price.

An example of how such a rate is arrived at follows. First the owner must determine the total cost of the project, as shown in Table 14-1.

DETERMINATION OF THE RATE

In Chapter 6 (Financing the Project) the entrepreneur is advised how to go about the initial financing of the project. At that time he has had to project a rental rate which will provide a return on his investment in time and money and will also provide a satisfactory and safe return to the lender.

The projected rent roll at that time is based on the final rentable square feet available in an office or other commercial structure or the price per room per month for a residential building. (Room count can be made by real estate board rules.)

At the time of renting the owner should know almost exactly what the project will cost, and he then can project the operating costs accurately. He must then add the total operating cost including taxes,

TABLE 14-1   COSTS TO BE INCLUDED IN DETERMINING TOTAL COST OF PROJECT

Total cost
  Price paid for original structure
    Closing costs, legal fees, administrative expense
    Cost of portion of taxes, water rates, fuel, etc., paid at closing by new owners or refunded by existing owner
  Cost of recycling
    Construction cost, including tenant work
    Architect's and engineer's fees
    Costs of permits and other filing fees
    Legal and administrative costs
    Insurance during construction
    Taxes during construction
    Cost of obtaining mortgage and other financing
    Interest on mortgage or other funds during construction
  Operating cost
    Taxes (real estate, water, sewage, improvement, etc.)
    Cost of maintenance and repair; payroll; supplies
    Contracts for cleaning, elevator maintenance, exterminating, etc.
    Cost of utilities and fuel
    Cost of tenant services called for by lease
    Brokerage fees and rental commissions
    Administrative and legal expense
    Insurance
    Management fee
  Mortgage interest and amortization
  Equity investment
    Required return on money investment*

---

*The time and money spent in the actual planning, construction, and promotion of the project should be taken care of in the construction cost, architect's fee, administrative costs, etc.

the interest and amortization on mortgage or other financing, and the required return on his equity.

The total should then be divided by the gross rentable square feet or rentable rooms. To the resulting number, which will be in dollars per square foot or per rentable room, he should add 5 percent for vacancies. This final figure is what he should obtain as the annual rent per unit of measurement (as an example $7.50 per square foot, or $1200 per room). He should now compare this figure with the going rents for space he considers competitive.

When the owner arrives at the rental he can charge, he must go through one other calculation. The commercial space may contain street-level stores or other space which rent at a different rate than office space. He must calculate the rent for each space so that the average rent will be $7.50 per square foot. For residential space he must price the various apartments by location, by size of rooms, and by the equipment installed and again arrive at the average rent ($1200 per room).

If the resultant rental seems too high to be competitive, the owner must cut some costs, e.g., by dropping extras he thought he could add to the construction cost, by eliminating some marginal services, or by lowering the rate of return on his own investment, until the building becomes well enough rented to permit the rental on the remaining space to be increased without danger to the investment. Rentals can be increased at renewal time or can be increased as the renting progresses.

15

RECYCLING

FOR A

CONDOMINIUM

15-1 PROBLEMS PECULIAR TO A CONDOMINIUM

In recycling a structure for a final use as a condominium, the developer must realize that he is building for potential home owners who will have a more severe set of standards than the renter. They will know that they are making a large investment, that they will have to carry a mortgage and pay real estate taxes, and that they will have to maintain the property at their own expense. There will be no landlord to complain to: *they* will be the landlord.

The original structure must therefore lend itself to conversion into individual units which can be sharply defined, and the recycler must pay more attention to attractive architecture and room arrangement and sturdy maintenance-free construction. This chapter is not about the conversion of existing apartment buildings to condominiums, a recent trend, because they are not recyclings but simply refinancings.

15-2   THE MARKET FOR CONDOMINIUMS

If the entrepreneur has decided he wishes to have a condominium as a final use, he must look for a certain type of building and location. A great many condominiums are now being sold to singles or to childless working couples. They should therefore be convenient to mass transportation or at least a short automobile ride from places where people work. The sizes of the units should also be tailored to this market, and there should be many of two and three rooms. At least two types of older structures lend themselves to this kind of recycling, the older garden-type apartments, which are widely scattered through the outskirts and near suburbs of all larger communities, and the large, well-built mansion located in a no longer fashionable residential area. Many of these have been broken up into a number of single-room apartments, usually illegally. Such buildings often have a special appeal that can make their conversion financially attractive.

In cities there are many old loft buildings which can be converted into attractive condominiums. A former brewery was recycled into office building and condominium apartments. Our first case study (Chap. 17) is of an old granite warehouse, which was recycled into a very successful apartment condominium. As a matter of fact, there are very few buildings which ingenuity and architectural imagination cannot convert into an office or apartment condominium or a combination of both.

15-3   FINANCIAL AND CONSTRUCTION CONSIDERATIONS

As will be shown in Sec. 15-4, the legal and other preparatory work involved in the creation of a condominium is much greater and more expensive than that for a rental project. Also, because of stricter construction inspections by the mortgagors, and because condominium purchasers have been told to be wary, the developer must be more careful about the quality of his work. The extra work, however, can be more than paid for by the profitability. The developer sells the units to individuals who assume the mortgage, the taxes, and the maintenance burdens. In a successful venture he ends up free and clear of all responsibilities (except for certain guaranties) and with a substantial profit on his investment.

15-4   HOW A CONDOMINIUM IS ESTABLISHED

Because of the history of abuses in condominium development and sales the federal government and the various states have promulgated rules and regulations (with the force of law) to protect the condominium purchaser. Some states have gone almost to the point of severely inhibiting condominium construction, but such laws can and will eventually be changed to provide a more even balance. The condominium regulation of Virginia is a case in point.

A condominium cannot be established until the property is purchased and at least preliminary plans are prepared. After this the entrepreneur must go through a number of additional rather complicated steps. It is strongly recommended that an attorney who is expert in condominium law and financing be retained.

A master deed must be prepared and recorded with the appropriate public authority, which dedicates the property to a condominium plan of ownership. This deed must be accompanied by:

The plan of the project

An accurate description of the various units

An accurate description of the common areas

The valuation and proportioned interest of each unit

The proposed by-laws of the association of the prospective owners

An absolute statement that the owner will not retain any ownership of the common facilities or of any facility that would inhibit the resale rights of the owners of the units

It is recommended that the developer and others contemplating a condominium obtain the federal[1] and the state regulations regarding such projects. Various states place condominiums under different divisions, but the department of state or commerce should know where the information can be obtained.

15-5   FINANCING A CONDOMINIUM

Mortgage with FHA Insurance

If the promotor or sponsor of a condominium is willing to go through the extra work and expense and can spare the additional time, he can

[1]Department of Housing and Urban Development (HUD), Washington, DC 20410.

try to obtain an FHA mortgage insurance commitment. Such a commitment almost automatically assures the sponsor that he will be able to obtain a mortgage from a financial institution. If the FHA route is chosen, the owner must first file the master deed with them (see Sec. 15-4). After this deed is filed, FHA makes a feasibility study; if this study shows that the project has a good chance of success, a certificate of insurance will be issued. Such a study serves to reassure the owner and is welcomed by the lender. The FHA insurance will also carry through to the individual owners, who can also be assured that they can obtain a mortgage.

Conventional Mortgage

Many insurance companies, savings banks, and building and loan associations welcome applications for condominium blanket loans because such loans give them entree to the individual purchasers of the units. They require the same master deed information as FHA but are likely to be less strict in some of their requirements. One of the important ones is the strict FHA rule about owner's use of down payments. There are others, but the experienced attorney should know what they are and guide the owner accordingly.

16

RECYCLING

UNDER HUD-FHA

SECTION 8

Within the scope of the National Housing Act of 1949, as amended, the U.S. Department of Housing and Urban Development together with FHA is authorized to make grants for the rehabilitation of residential structures in certain areas. Loans for the rehabilitation of such residential structures are authorized under Section 312 of the Housing Act of 1964, as amended. The entire program of grants, FHA-insured loans, rent subsidies, etc., is generally known as Section 8. Its basic purpose is to provide clean, safe, modern housing in depressed areas for those people (low income, minorities, the elderly, or others) who could not afford or otherwise qualify for conventional housing.

This chapter, which is for the information of an entrepreneur who may be an investor, an attorney, a developer, a builder, an architect-engineer, or a combination of any of these, outlines the necessary procedures for entering into the field of recycling underutilized or abandoned tenements or similar structures into livable dwelling units with the help of an FHA-insured mortgage, subsidized rents, and with IRS tax benefits on the return on equity. If the entrepreneur is solely an investor, he must employ an attorney, an architect-engineer, a builder, and a building-management company. A much more successful and more competitive situation can be created by the entrepreneur who combines one or more of these necessary functions as in-house subsidiaries. The federal agencies who must pass on applications and subsidies for such housing are sympathetic to entrepreneurs who are competitive enough to require lower mortgages and subsidies. Many successful combinations of management and construction firms, architect and investors, or others are now in the business.

The start and successful completion of such a project requires a substantial amount of seed money, which is in fact required by FHA-HUD before an application can be processed.[1] The money is required (1) to purchase the building or leasehold (sometimes from the municipal authority which has probably foreclosed it for taxes), (2) to employ an attorney who is knowledgeable in this field, (3) to employ an architect-engineer to design the rehabilitation, and (4) to furnish the difference between the usual 90 percent insured permanent mortgage and the total cost of the project. Interim construction financing is required, and such money is advanced as the recycling progresses. Under agreement between the federal and local authority such projects are tax-abated.

When the project is completed, it is occupied by low-income tenants and receives substantial federal rent subsidies which can be renegotiated if necessary if the income falls short of the expense. The project has to be managed by a professional real estate management firm, which may be asked to train a certain number of minority members as submanagers, handymen, etc. The management firm collects the rents and the subsidy, pays the mortgage interest and amortization, pays all salaries and maintenance charges, and banks the difference (if any) for subsequent distribution.

Certain basic requirements must be complied with before an FHA guarantee can be issued:

The project must be located on real estate held in fee simple or subject to a lease of at least 75 years from the date of the mortgage.

The property must consist of five or more units.

Commercial facilities may not exceed 10 percent of the gross floor area and commercial income not more than 15 percent of the gross rent roll.

---

[1] If a project is not approved by FHA, some of this seed money may be lost.

HUD-FHA will allow a maximum rental sufficient to allow the entrepreneur a fair return on his investment which is exclusive of tax benefits and depreciation.

The sponsor can have a further advantage by using such a project as a tax shelter.

A feasibility survey by the sponsor is also required. Such a study must include the need for the project, the marketability of his particular project, the zoning, and the economic feasibility, which includes total cost, maintenance, and the level of rents sufficient to produce a return on the investment. One basic requirement reads, "The sponsor is thoroughly knowledgeable and has a record of proven capability for producing economically sound projects." The architect and contractor must also be able to prove records of successful design and completion of work within a budget.

The terms of the mortgage provide that if the mortgagor suffers an operating loss in the first 2 years, the amount of the insured mortgage may be increased by an amount equal to 90 percent of the overrun. There are also certain covenants such as a prohibition against the use of the premises for any other purpose than that originally contemplated and a prohibition against any liens other than the FHA mortgage.

The construction contracts must comply with all government regulations regarding prevailing wages and equal employment opportunity, and the work is subject to government inspection. The contractor is also allowed a fee for overhead and profit. There is also a provision that when there is an "identity of interest" between the builder and the sponsor, there will be a 10 percent allowance for profit based on the total construction cost. When the sponsor or mortgagor has no identity of interest with the contractor, he is allowed a profit of 10 percent based on the architect's fee, the carrying charges and financing, legal and organizational costs, and allowable off-site costs. This is one illustration of the extra profit that can be obtained by the formation of an identity of interest between the sponsor (mortgagor) and the contractor.

There is also a program [221(d)4] which allows a profit-motivated sponsor to provide low-rent housing thorough long-term lease arrangements with local housing authorities.

The procedure necessary to obtain a Section 8 HUD-FHA mortgage commitment, subsequent rent subsidies, and other benefits is a good deal more complicated than this simple outline might indicate, but it can provide very definite benefits for the sophisticated investor.

The program was designed to provide social benefits while at the same time making it profitable for an entrepreneur to do so.

17

CASE STUDY ONE:
LEWIS WHARF,
BOSTON, MASSACHUSETTS

17-1 INTRODUCTION AND GENERAL DESCRIPTION

The recycling of Lewis Wharf on the Boston waterfront can be considered as a historical preservation as well as a profit-making venture. The granite warehouse and the Pilot House, which are the subjects of this study, are fine examples of the architecture of New England in the early nineteenth century. Boston at that time was one of the prime seaports on the east coast. Ships put into Boston from every port in the world, and Lewis Wharf was strategically located to receive cargoes and send them on by rail to all parts of this country. This kind of activity required warehousing, and in 1836 a group of Boston businessmen began the construction of the granite warehouse, which was completed in 1840. It was the finest warehouse on the waterfront. It was from here that the clipper ships *Flying Cloud, Fearless,* and others sailed to San Francisco, China, and Australia.

In 1966, Carl Koch, FAIA, a well-known Boston architect, was looking for new office space because his office on Harvard Square had to be vacated. Koch was drawn to the Boston waterfront, which at that time was a dreary melange of rundown buildings, littered streets, abandoned or partly used warehouses, and small factories. He could see beyond this and envision how the area would look if it were restored. At this time, also, the Boston Redevelopment Authority was being formed, with broad authority to take over property by eminent domain and to control growth patterns.

Koch was impressed by the sturdiness and architectural integrity of the granite warehouse and the Pilot House (Fig. 17-1). He formed the Boston Waterfront Development Corp. and in 1966 purchased Lewis Wharf for $1.195 million. Since that time Koch and his associates have planned, built, financed, and marketed a landmark recycling which adds immeasurably to the historic Boston waterfront but which in addition (and most importantly) shows every prospect of being a profitable investment (Fig. 17-2).

At this writing the 18,000 ft^2 of basement space in 65 percent rented and the 25,900 ft^2 first-floor retail space in the Granite Building is 75 percent rented. The 30,000 ft^2 of second-floor office space is 100

FIGURE 17-1   Original building, with part of Boston fishing fleet in foreground.

FIGURE 17-2   View of recycled building.

percent rented, and the 102,000 ft² of residential condominiums on the third to sixth floors are all sold. (There are 93 condominium units, ranging from one to three bedrooms.)

The Pilot House office space is 100 percent rented, and the first-floor restaurant is in full and prosperous operation. There are still financial and operating problems to be solved, but the superb location and the ambience of the project assure success.

Following is a detailed study of how it was done. The order of headings will follow insofar as possible the chapter headings of this book.

17-2   MARKETING SURVEY

Carl Koch, the architect and the leadman of the recycling effort, was looking for an office location on the waterfront when he was given the opportunity to purchase Lewis Wharf. Before he could enlist financial support for the purchase, his first step had to be a marketing survey. For what purpose could the property be used that would be profitable, would preserve its architectural integrity to the greatest extent possible, and would appeal to Boston as a leader in the rehabilitation of its historic waterfront? He was helped in his decision by the unique location. It is only a short walk from the heart of Boston's office-building, financial, government, and historic center. Yet it is tucked away from the noise and heavy traffic of the city. It is only a few minutes' walk from a subway station which connects to greater Boston's transportation network. Yet the walk to the station is through a park located on the waterfront. It is only a short distance from the South Station of the railroad and a short taxi ride from the airport. It is under the aegis of a redevelopment authority whose prime purpose is to restore and beautify the entire area and which has given a sample of its intentions by the development of a large waterfront park just two streets from the site.

And with all these advantages of location it is surrounded by boat basins, has a wide view of the harbor, and is only a few hundred yards from one of the harbor's main ship channels.

Two other surveys were made before the decision what to build was arrived at. While a survey of the city as a whole was not really necessary in this case because the participants in the project were prominent local businessmen, the following example of a city survey is worth including here. It was made by the Mortgage Department of the Equitable Life Assurance Society of the United States before it became the holder of the permanent financing.

Site Data

The subject site consists of a total of 3.66 acres of land and piers divided into five parcels as shown on the plot plan (Fig. 17-3). It fronts on Atlantic Avenue, a wide thoroughfare at the Boston waterfront, and extends to a granite seawall on the east. It also extends from the present Eastern Avenue on the north to a bulkhead at the water's edge on the south. The site is generally level. All utilities are available, including electricity, gas, water, telephone, and storm- and sanitary-sewer connections to the city sewer system.

Economic Base

Boston is the world center of nuclear, electronic, and medical science. It is the center of the commercial, financial, wholesale, and retail trade and service activities not only for the Boston metropolitan area but for all New England. It is the major market and distribution point for raw materials and manufactured products for this highly industrialized area, the center of the fishing industry, and one of the major seaports on the Atlantic Coast. It is the largest wool market in the nation. In 1971 the Massachusetts Division of Employment Security reported 17,683

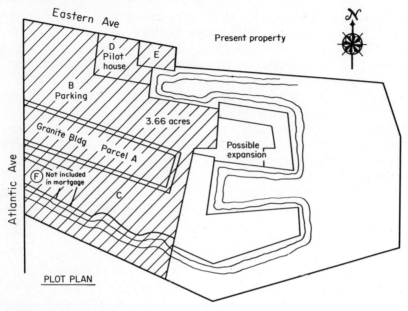

FIGURE 17-3 Plot plan.

firms in Boston with an average of 360,247 total employees and with an annual payroll of $3,018,440,128. Wholesale and retail trade, with 30.5 percent of the total number of employees reported and 25.9 percent of the total annual payroll, was the leading industry as measured by both employment and payrolls.

Identity of the Property

The subject property is known as the Lewis Wharf Development of the Boston Waterfront Development Corporation. It is located at and near 28 Atlantic Avenue on the Boston waterfront and comprises five parcels of land and piers totaling 3.66 acres, with certain buildings situated thereon and more particularly identified as follows (see Fig. 17-3):

> *Parcel A.* those condominium units comprising the second floor, ground floor, and basement space (containing 30,033 rentable square feet of office space, 25,889 rentable square feet of commercial or retail space, and 18,010 rentable square feet of storage or commercial space, respectively) being a part of the six-story Granite Building situated on 0.86 acre of land.

Parcel B.   approximately 1.19 acres of land to be used for parking and landscaped areas, and situated between Atlantic Avenue and the existing seawall.

Parcel C.   approximately 1 acre of land surrounding Parcel A and to be used for access and landscaping.

Parcel D.   approximately 0.29 acre improved with a 5½-story and basement brick building, known as the Pilot House, containing approximately 34,955 ft² of rentable office and restaurant space.

Parcel E.   approximately 0.11 acre of land adjoining the Pilot House on the east and to be used for landscaping.

Parcel F.   approximately 0.21 acre of land to be improved with a two-story building containing 11,108 ft² of restaurant space, including renovation of portions of an existing structure.

Transportation

Boston is New England's leading seaport, a regional rail, bus, and truck terminal center and an important air transport center.

RAIL

Boston is the terminus of two trunk-line railroads, the Boston and Maine and Conrail. The Boston and Maine serves cities and towns north of Boston and west to Worcester. Conrail goes west through the central part of the state to Worcester, Springfield, Pittsfield, and into Albany, New York. This railroad also provides passenger and freight service to points south and southwest of Boston. These two railroads also provide commuter service between Boston and surrounding municipalities and thus are an important part of the Massachusetts transportation system.

HIGHWAYS

The city is literally a hub from which many highways serving the city extend to the north, west, and south. Route 128, Boston's circumferential highway, interchanges with many highways feeding into the city.

Massachusetts Turnpike (Interstate Route 90), the most important highway out of the city, crosses Route 128 in Weston and terminates in West Stockbridge, with an extension to the New York Thruway.

17-3 NEIGHBORHOOD SURVEY

When completed, this area will complement the entire city and create a revitalized downtown Boston where old and new are effectively merged to maintain the character of a historic city in a modern era.

Notwithstanding the historical and aesthetic aspects of the subject location and neighborhood, the site is also ideal from a purely practical standpoint. Transportation facilities are excellent, with the Callahan Tunnel entrance and Fitzgerald Expressway, only three blocks away, providing express highway access in all directions. The city railroad terminals and Logan International Airport are within minutes by car. The central high-rise office district and retail area are about three to five blocks southwest and within easy walking distance.

Residents of the waterfront area tend to be relatively affluent business people with offices in either the wharf areas, the financial district, or Government Center. Over 62 percent of waterfront households have incomes over $15,000 compared with 25 percent for the city as a whole. Accordingly, about 68 percent of waterfront residents are in professional or technical occupations and are, therefore, largely highly educated.

Office tenants in this area are not limited to any particular category of business, while the retail tenants tend to be specialty shops, boutiques, art and handicraft galleries, restaurants, and cafes.

In summary, the subject enjoys a location and neighborhood which is ideal and unique in all aspects for office use, specialty retail, and urban residential.

Local Transportation

Buses run along Atlantic Avenue for several blocks between North and South Stations, passing the subject property. The Aquarium stop on the MTA (subway) is just two blocks south at the corner of Atlantic and State Streets. The MTA provides subway service to all of Boston and its nearby towns.

Entrance to the John Fitzgerald Expressway, the major North-South artery through Boston, is just several blocks away. This main artery connects with all major highways to the north and south and with the Massachusetts Turnpike to the west.

17-4   DETERMINING THE ULTIMATE USE

The survey of the neighborhood almost directly indicates the most successful final objective of the recycling. The use falls into five categories.

1. Residential condominiums in a combination of one-, two-, and three-bedroom units for singles, working couples, weekend sailors, and city-oriented residents in general (Figs. 17-4 and 17-5).

2. Office space that can be divided for small users. It would appeal to tenants who would like a prestige address without being lost in a major downtown office building.

3. Shops of the boutique type (Fig. 17-6) that would cater to tourists and greater Boston residents who could wander down from Faneuil Hall, Quincy Market, and the Government Center to visit the waterfront.

4. Restaurants that take advantage of the site. Seafood, special

FIGURE 17-4   Typical apartment.

FIGURE 17-5 Typical apartment.

decorations, large glass area, special gimmicks (a free carafe of wine, a lush salad bar).

5. A parking lot for all these activities.

17-5 FORMING THE RECYCLING TEAM

Koch enlisted the support of prominent businessmen and between them they formed the Boston Waterfront Development Corporation, made up as follows:

Carl Koch, FAIA, architect and leadman

Edward Mank, prominent Boston real estate developer

Gregory Bemis, an investor

David Heilner, an investor with experience in real estate

John Bok, an attorney who was formerly General Counsel for the Redevelopment Authority and who was involved in condominium law and in major rehabilitation projects

FIGURE 17-6 Retail flower shop.

James Craig, a former officer of a major hotel chain whose expertise
was in planning and development and who was to be in
charge of planning, building, and managing the project

17-6 HOW THE DECISION WAS MADE

The Real Estate Consultant

TREND

The subject's ideal location with relation to the prime downtown financial and retail districts, the Government Center, the North End, and
indeed all of Boston, its historical background, its successful and con-
tinuing rehabilitation, and its commanding position as a waterfront
property close to the center city—all point to a favorable and continued
upward trend.

HIGHEST AND BEST USE

In view of the subject property's excellent waterfront site and its historical significance, together with its location within easy walking distance of Boston's downtown Government Center complex and principal office, banking, and retail areas, the proposed development as described represents an optimum use of the subject land in accordance with the zoning and objectives of the Urban Renewal Plan.

LAND COMPARISONS

Various parcels of land in the waterfront redevelopment area have been sold at prices pegged by the Boston Redevelopment Authority, but research and inquiry has revealed no open-market sales of sites similar to the subject property. Therefore the appraisers have assembled data on other BRA sales of land in the waterfront area and investigated sales of office building and commercial sites in the downtown Boston area, primarily on the basis of floor area, as a guide to the land value of the subject property (Table 17-1). Land sales in Boston involving sites suitable for office or commercial use reportedly vary according to allowable density, with typical prices starting at about $5 per square foot of potential building area. For example, high-density sites permitting a floor-area ratio of 10 (10 × the land area) sell for $50 per square foot of land and up. Similarly, low-density sites, such as the subject land, with allowable floor area in the vicinity of 2 to 1 typically sell for $10 per square foot of land.

RENT COMPARISONS

Rent comparisons of the type shown in Table 17-2 were made for office space, and the same type of comparison was made for condominium prices, retail stores, restaurants, and parking lots.

The Architect-Engineer Team

The input of the architect-engineer team is an integral part of the decision-making process. The existing structure must be evaluated, and the improvements should be designed to take full advantage of it. The structural, mechanical, and electrical details and interior and exterior finishes should be designed so that the least amount of cutting, patching, and rebuilding is necessary. In this case a team was formed consisting of a structural engineer, a mechanical engineer, and an

TABLE 17-1 LAND SALES BY BOSTON REDEVELOPMENT AUTHORITY

Identification	Location	Sale date	Owner	Area, ft²	Price, $/ft²	Improvements	Comment
Small parcel at front of Parcel A2 in Downtown Urban Renewal Area acquired for addition to site of Harbor Towers Apartments	Atlantic Ave., several blocks south of subject	Jan., 1969	T. Berenson	71,300	$4.60	High-rise rental apartments	Sale made in 1969, when plans for subject area not nearly so far advanced as now; subject site considered equal or better; upward adjustment necessary for time
Site of Harbor Towers parking garage, Parcel A3 in Downtown Waterfront Urban Renewal Area	Milk St. and Atlantic Ave., several blocks south of subject	Jan., 1969	T. Berenson	53,400	$5.50	Multilevel parking garage	Sale now dated; subject considered better

TABLE 17-2 RENT COMPARISONS WITH OTHER OFFICE SPACE

Property	Description	Size, rentable ft²	Rental rate, $/ft²	Other rental conditions	Comment
Commercial Wharf West (across Atlantic Ave.)	Similar to subject but not waterfront	8000	$7	Tenant pays for electricity, and owner pays for heat and air conditioning	Subject much superior
Long Wharf (waterfront, next to Chart House Restaurant)	On pier south of subject	....	$6	Plus utility charges and tax escalation	Subject much better
Atlantic Ave.	Small office space in vicinity	....	$6.50–$7		Subject much superior
Three Center Plaza Building	Last of three 9-story Center Plaza buildings in downtown Government Center, completed 1969, about five blocks west of subject	200,000	$7.50–$11*		Better overall than subject

*Original rentals in 1969.

electrical engineer. The first building to be considered was the Granite Building.

The first step was to determine the maximum rentable area for the commercial space and the maximum salable area for the condominiums. These figures are given in Table 17-3. The next step was to survey the structure.

THE SURVEY OF THE STRUCTURE

When the original purchase of the Granite Building was made, Koch was given a set of plans which were fairly complete and which showed the original structure of the building. These plans had been prepared by the former owner from actual measurements taken of the existing structure. They were structural only. There were no mechanical or electrical plans because in modern times the building had been only partially occupied and for less important commercial uses. There was no electrical or mechanical installation that could be of any use in a modern building.

The foundations   It was known that the original building had been built on a clay coffer dam which rested on timber piles. The outer walls were of granite block and the basement area was separated by heavy brick masonry walls into a series of bays which carry all the way up through the structure to the top of the fourth floor.

The walls were examined for seepage and for cracks. There were none. The integrity of the supporting piles was vouched for by the city of Boston. In excavating for sewer and water lines the city had partially uncovered some of the piles and found them in better than original condition since immersion in salt water had made them stone hard.

TABLE 17-3   RENTABLE AND SALABLE AREA OF GRANITE BUILDING

Floor	Use	Gross area, ft^2	Rentable or salable area, ft^2
Basement	Retail and storage, utilities	31,164	18,010
First	Shops and lobby	31,164	25,889
Second	Offices, corridor, toilets	31,164	30,033
Third through sixth	Residential condominiums*	124,656	124,656

*31,164 × 4 = 124,656.

The basement-area headroom was not sufficient for the installation of a heating or air-conditioning plant, and the first thought was that the mechanical plant would be placed on the roof. (This was subsequently changed; see final specifications below.)

Structural characteristics   The original structure was intact. It is of heavy mill construction with 14- by 14-in timbers bearing on the 18-in brick masonry walls that separate the bays. There were interior stairways in each bay and no communication between the bays. It was known that the loading of the structure had been as high as 300 lb/ft² with no signs of stress. It was therefore accepted that the floor loading called for by the present building code was well within the capacity of the structure.

The exterior wall   The exterior wall has preserved its integrity for well over 100 years. It is of 24-in-thick granite block backed by brick masonry. There were very few signs of leakage. The location of the window openings fitted the planned layout. The windows and frames were to be replaced.

Mechanical and electrical   As already noted, there was no existing installation of any significance. Sewer, water, and electrical feeder lines are in a strip of land immediately adjacent to the building under an easement, and so there was no problem about connections to public utilities.

Roof   The recycling scheme has used the structure of the first four floors of the building as it existed. The height of the present fifth and sixth floors however was taken up by a peaked roof with dormers cut into it. This was such an impractical use of space that the architect decided it must be replaced by a mansard roof, which would add almost two full floors of usable space.

Stairways and exits   No existing stairways or exit facilities were acceptable by any modern code and the architect had to plan completely new facilities before a building permit could be issued.

Adaptability of the structure for renovation   The 22-ft 6-in width between the masonry bays and the existing fenestration determined how the space had to be divided. Corridors running the length of the building would have to be opened up; such corridors (Fig. 17-7) would be 6 ft wide and provide two spaces in each bay each approximately 22

FIGURE 17-7   Arch cut through 18-ft brick bay wall and
typical corridor.

ft 6 in wide by 35 ft deep, which is quite acceptable office space and
which can be readily adapted for residential use.

The floor-to-floor clear heights are 7 ft 6 in for the basement, 9 ft
from the first to the second and 9 ft-6 in for the next two floors. This was
sufficient for everything but a basement mechanical plant.

Legal stairways and elevator and pipe shafts would have to be cut
through, but the floor construction was certainly sturdy enough for any
necessary framed openings.

In general the structure presented no very expensive or insur-
mountable difficulties in the way of recycling.

ZONING AND BUILDING-CODE REQUIREMENTS

Zoning   B4, Downtown Waterfront—Faneuil Hall Urban Renewal Plan,
permits a compatible mixture of residential use related to the waterfront and the old brick and granite buildings of the area and comple-

mentary types of offices and business occupants adding desirable commercial activity to the area. Preferred development is structures of moderate height, and the intention is to preserve the wharf-type waterfront motif for historical as well as urban-design purposes. Plans for the subject development have been approved by the Boston Redevelopment Authority.

The following copy of the minutes of the City of Boston, Board of Appeal, will give the prospective recycler an excellent idea of the kind of objections he is likely to get from the zoning and building departments and how, in this particular case, the architect overcame these objections.

Decision of the Board of Appeal on the Appeal of Boston Waterfront Development Corporation from the refusal of the Building Commissioner to grant a permit as the same would be in violation of Chapter 479 of the Acts of 1938, as amended, to wit:

Section 1700.0: In every store building each store shall have at least one (1) water closet and one (1) lavatory for the use of its tenant. Such a water closet shall not be accessible from an adjoining store (See sec. 10.13.8a of the State Plumbing Code).—The owner proposes to have common facilities for the tenants.

Section 221.2 Table 2-2: Buildings of type 3B construction of L2 occupancy are not allowed over 4 stories or 50 ft high.—The existing building is 5 stories and 71 ft high with a high pitched roof. The proposed structure will be 6 stories and 66.7 ft high.

Section 509.1.1: Kitchens more than 70 ft² in area shall have natural ventilation. Kitchens less than 70 ft² in area shall be ventilated by natural means or mechanical means exhausting at least 2 ft³/min of air per square foot of floor area.—Kitchen areas varying from 64.8 to 76.9 ft² are proposed to have ductless hoods. Larger kitchens will have a mechanical exhaust system. All kitchens are interior rooms.

Section 618.4.2: No winders shall be permitted in required exit stairways.—The stairs from the first floor to the basement in the stores are existing with winders.

Section 618.9: Required interior stairways shall be build with solid risers.—The proposed stairs will have open risers.

In connection with the specific variances sought, the following information was furnished:

Section 1700.0: The building will provide common facilities for the store tenants, including separate water closets and lavatories for men and women, each accessible from the common corridor. Since the stores are all small size, it would be impractical to provide separate facilities for each small store.

Section 221.2, Table 2-2: The existing building is five stories and 71 ft high in most parts, with a high-pitched roof. The proposed structure will be less tall, only 66.7 ft high, and six stories. The addition will be constructed of fireproof materials, and it would be impractical to remodel the building without making the additions on the roof floors.

Section 509.1.1: The kitchens for which the variances are required exceed the 70-ft^2 limitation by less than 10 percent. In addition all will have ductless hoods. Larger kitchens will meet the code and have a mechanical system. It would be a hardship to redesign the kitchens to make them less than 70 ft^2 or to require an expensive mechanical exhaust system for the smaller kitchens.

Section 618.4.2: The stairs from the first floor to the basement are within the store space and will be used only by the store personnel. They are not a required means of egress and it would be a hardship to require their rebuilding to eliminate the winders.

Section 618.9: Under the previously approved plans, the required interior staircases were of steel construction and ordered with open risers. The new code requires solid risers and was not to apply to this building until recently. It would be a substantial hardship to require the reordering and refabrication of these stairs.

Section 1207.1.a.2: The rehabilitated building is surrounded by a high-pressure fireline with hydrants and is accessible on three sides by fireboats. It is therefore not necessary to install a full standpipe system in order to provide adequate fire protection to the building and would be both difficult of installation and extremely expensive.

The Board is of the opinion that all conditions required for the granting of an order under section 119 and the sections above referred to have been met and that the varying of the terms of the building code outlined above will not conflict with the intent and spirit of the Building Code and would prevent a manifest injustice from being done.

Therefore, sitting under its discretionary power the Board, through its members and substitute members sitting in this appeal, unanimously vote to grant the variance as requested, to annul the refusal of the Building Commissioner and to order him to grant a permit in accordance with this request.

Signed October 24, 1972

LAND COVERAGE

1. Granite Building 31,164 ft^2 on 37,461 ft^2 of land allotted to it by the plot plans (83%)

2. Granite Building, Pilot House, and one other building (Rosebud) that has not yet been developed: 50,328 ft² building area on 159,430 ft² land (32%)

Easements and Encroachments   A 20-ft-wide utility easement (gas, electric, water,and sewer) runs from Atlantic Ave. eastward on the north side of the Granite Building, then southward on its east side.

Building code requirements   Salient points of the Boston Building Code which refer specifically to this project can be paraphrased as follows.

Sections 105 and 106 state that the existing use and occupancy of a structure cannot be changed without compliance with the new basic code. They also state that if a structure is altered within any 12-month period at a cost of more than 50 percent of its physical value, it must comply with the new basic code. As this project comes within both of these sections, the recycling has to comply in all respects with the new code.

INCOME AND EXPENSE

See Table 17-4.

Condominium common charge   As stated in the condominium documents, unit owners are responsible for common charges of the condominium in proportion to their respective percentages of beneficial interest. As it is set up now, the common charges of the condominium include gas heat for the entire building, i.e., common areas and individual units; electricity for the entire building except for the basement, ground floor, and exterior lighting, which is paid by individual retail tenants; water and sewer charges; contracts for elevator maintenance, air-conditioning maintenance, pest control, and television system maintenance; insurance; and miscellaneous items and repairs. The residential portion of the condominium is responsible for 63.3 percent of the common charges, and the commercial portion of the condominium is responsible for 36.7 percent of the common charges.

ESTIMATED INCOME FOR PARCEL B, PARKING LOT

The capacity of the lot, according to its presently proposed use, will be 210 parking spaces, increased to 250 spaces during peak hours, using some aisle space and taking into consideration a permanent-access easement over adjoining Parcel C.

Condominium owners are entitled to a limited number of parking

TABLE 17-4 INCOME AND EXPENSE FOR PARCEL A, GRANITE BUILDING

Rental income:*
  Office space (second floor):

Gross income, 33,033 ft² at $8.25	$248,000	
Vacancy and rent loss, 3%	7,500	
Effective gross income (EGI)		$240,500

  Retail space (ground floor):

Gross income, 25,889 ft² at $8.50	$220,000	
Vacancy and rent loss, 7%	15,500	
EGI		204,500

  Commercial and storage space
  (basement):

Gross income, 18,010 ft² at $3.45	$ 62,000	
Vacancy and rent loss, 10%	6,200	
EGI		55,800
Total EGI		$500,800 say $501,000

Expenses for commercial portion of building:
  Common charges† for residential
  condominiums and commercial
  space:

Gas	$ 30,000	
Electricity	42,000	
Water and sewer	10,000	
Wages	41,500	
Management	24,000	
Contracts	9,000	
Insurance	14,000	
Pool	47,000	
Miscellaneous and repairs	15,000	
Expenses for commercial space:	$235,500 say	$230,000
Condominium common charge		
(commerical part)	$ 84,410	
Cleaning, 30,033 ft² at $0.50	15,017	
Repairs and maintenance, 73,932		
ft² at $0.05	3,700	
Management, 3% EGI	15,000	
Contingency	1,800	
	$119,927‡	
Real estate taxes, 23% of $501,000		
EGI	115,230§	
		$235,157 say $235,000

Net income before recapture	$266,000

---

*The third to sixth floors are condominiums. The owners of these units share in certain common expenses but pay their own taxes and financing charges.

†These charges as divided as follows:

Residential, 63.3% × $230,000	$145,000
Commercial, 36.7% × $230,000	84,410
100%	$230,000

‡$1.62 per square foot.

§$1.55 per square foot.

spaces on this parcel (and/or Parcel C) at $35 per month each. There are 94 apartment units, and the sponsors are entitled to 60 spaces for office tenants and 15 spaces for retail tenants. The number of permanent spaces reserved on this basis is estimated at 165, with the remaining 85 spaces being used by 200 patrons per day at an average of 50 cents each, or a turnover of these spaces about 2⅓ times per day, producing income of slightly over $1 per day per car space for these 85 spaces. This does not allow for possible use by the operator of the spaces of permanent parking tenants during their absence, which is permissible.

Transients in the area per day due to Lewis Wharf only are estimated at 1325 as follows:

Patrons of restaurants	1250
Office visitors	30
Visitors by auto to retail establishments	35
Visitors to apartments, marina, etc.	10
	1325

The income and expenses of the subject parcel are therefore conservatively estimated as shown in Table 17-5.

The owners have a contract with Pilgrim Parking, Inc., to operate the parking facility for 7 percent of gross receipts less expenses, which is included in the above 25 percent operating expense. The owners and others knowledgeable in the field agree that 25 percent of gross income is a realistic and reasonable estimate of operating expenses for parking.

TABLE 17-5 ESTIMATED ANNUAL INCOME AND EXPENSES FOR PARCEL B

Income:			
Residential condominiums	90		
Office tenants	60		
Retail tenants	15		
Permanent spaces	165 at $35 per month	$5775 per month	
Transients, 200 per day at $0.50 average × 30 days		3000	
Total monthly income		$8775	
Annual income ($8775 × 12)			$105,300
Expenses:			
Operating, 25%	$26,325		
Contingency	5,000		
Taxes (23% of gross)	24,219		
Total expenses (53%)		say	55,300
Net income			$ 50,000

lots similar to the subject. A contingency of $5000 is added. As usual in Boston, real estate taxes are estimated at 23 percent of effective gross income.

PARCEL C

This parcel will be unimproved at first, except with landscaped walkways and a bowling green on the south side of the Granite Building and some parking on the north and east sides of the building. The north portion of this parcel is also subject to a permanent easement for access and parking. Thus it will be essentially non-income-producing. The condominium owners and tenants have the right to use the bowling green for a small charge. The east end of this parcel may later be used for additional parking, if needed, and it is understood that except for the bowling green, this parcel could be used for retail kiosks or other such development. However, its size and shape obviously would not accommodate an intensive-use development, such as an office building. Actually, because of its physical pattern and relationship to Parcel A, Parcel C belongs with Parcel A, the condominium site.

Because of its physical layout and limited use, Parcel C is valued, by comparison with other BRA land sales, at $200,000, or $4.60 per ft^2.

PARCELS D AND E

These two parcels, containing a total of 0.40 acre, or 17,424 ft^2, are considered together as the site of the Pilot House. The Pilot House, as previously described, will contain 34,955 rentable square feet, including 11,620 ft^2 of restaurant space on ground floor and basement, and 23,335 ft^2 of office space on the third through fifth floors and the fifth-floor mezzanine. The rents are stabilized as shown in Table 17-6 and are in line with the market.

PARCEL F

The building on the approximately 0.23 acre of land is to be completely renovated as a restaurant, which will contain 11,085 ft^2. At this writing no firm lease has been signed.

The net income from this property is estimated at $71,000 per annum based on a minimum guaranteed rent of $90,000. The income can rise to $100,000 if the projected percentage rentals (7.5 percent down to 7.0 percent) are fulfilled. These figures are based on continuing negotiations.

TABLE 17-6   ESTIMATED INCOME AND EXPENSE FOR PARCELS D AND E

Gross income:

Restaurant space, 11,620 ft² at $8.69			$100,990
Office space:			
Second floor,	5108 ft² at $ 9.70	$49,548	
Third floor,	5108 ft² at 9.30	47,504	
Fourth floor,	5108 ft² at 9.25	47,250	
Fifth floor,*	8011 ft² at 10.00	80,010	
			224,310
Total gross income			$325,300
Vacancy allowance, 4.2% (7% restaurant, 3% office)			13,800
EGI			$311,500
Estimated expenses:			
Management, 3%		$ 9,350	
Payroll		8,000	
Gas, heat		5,600	
Electricity		7,900	
Water and sewer tax		700	
Cleaning		11,700	
Decorating		950	
Building repair		1,400	
Elevator maintenance		1,350	
Insurance, $0.09/ft²		3,100	
Miscellaneous		950	
Real estate taxes, 23% of EGI		71,670	
			122,645†
Net income before recapture			$188,855

*Includes fifth-floor mezzanine.

†Total expenses can be broken down as follows:

Operating expenses, per ft²	$1.45	$ 51,000
Real estate taxes, per ft²	2.05	71,650
Total	$3.50	$122,650

THE FINAL PLANS AND SPECIFICATIONS

The final plans and specifications from which the Granite Building (the principal structure on Lewis Wharf) was recycled are summarized below.

Demolition

All exterior fire escapes

All interior plaster or covering on bearing walls

All floor covering other than wood

All ceiling covering (expose timbers)

All stairwells (these were within the bays)

All timber floor structures at new stair and elevator shafts

Cut openings through all masonry walls that separate bays to provide for a 6-ft-wide corridor to run the length of the building

Existing elevator-shaft walls and equipment

All utility systems except main house plumbing drains and any potentially usable wastes and vents

Site work and landscaping   As the Granite Building occupied almost all the land area allotted to it, the site work refers to adjacent parcels, which are all part of the Lewis Wharf complex. Asphalt paving with parking for 210 cars will be available on an adjoining parcel or parcels of land. Railroad ties will provide curbing in the parking areas. Walkways on the south, east, and north sides of the building vary from 5 to 8 ft in width and consist of sections of brick pavers set in sand, granite pavers set in sand, and aggregate concrete. On adjoining land (Parcel C) on the south side of the building is a 4800 ft² bowling green and several gardens containing various plantings which are connected by peastone walkways. This area will also contain plantings of several varieties of trees and shrubs, cobblestone walkways, and park benches.

Site utilities   This specification is separated from the plumbing and is treated as a separate trade because it involves the rehabilitation and repair of existing utilities that go beyond the normal obligations of a plumbing contractor. It involves the repair and rebuilding to present requirements of storm sewers, sanitary sewers, manholes, catch basins, and water lines, which are located at a distance of 10 ft or more from the building line. It involves masonry and piping and miscellaneous iron as well as excavation and backfill.

Cast-in-place concrete   All new grade beams, elevator and incinerator structures, and mechanical-space bounding walls are specified to be of 3000 lb/in² reinforced concrete. Roof fill to be of lightweight concrete. A cast-concrete floor slab is specified for the new fifth floor. Flooring of new balconies to be of 5000 lb/in² reinforced concrete. All existing plank floors to be covered with 2 in of concrete brought to a true, plane finish.

Stair landings to be of 3000 lb/in² reinforced concrete and steel-pan stairs to be filled with concrete and brought to a true troweled finish.

Masonry and granite work   Many of the residential units have projecting balconies; to make them accessible the window openings located at
these balconies had to be cut to accommodate doors. This necessitated
new granite returns and sills and new backup masonry. The specification mentions the granite quarry to be used and calls for close
matching.

It also calls for new granite sills, jambs, and lintels at new window
openings, which had to be cut into the east wall. All the openings cut
through the masonry bay walls were to be patched and trimmed with
matching material.

The specification also mentions fireplace work for the residential
units consisting of fire brick, slate hearths, and flue-pipe work.

Structural steel   The two-story mansard-roofed addition, which took
the place of the original peaked roof, was specified to be framed with
structural steel. Open-web steel joists are supported by steel columns
and girders.

Stairs   The stairs come under the "miscellaneous iron" specification.
They are specified to be 14-gauge steel-pan stairs, platforms, and
landings and steel railings. The stairway schedule is as follows:

Number	Run
3	Basement to roof
1	Basement to sixth floor
1	Basement to ground, heavy timber

There are also specifications for stairways to give access from first-floor
shops to basement areas, installed at tenant's request.

Framing and rough carpentry   The heavy mill construction of the
original structure was found in excellent condition so that the specification confines itself to cutting and framing openings for utilities,
elevators, stairs, and flues and closing existing openings, which had
been used for intercommunicating stairs in the bays and for interior
hoistways.

Finish carpentry   This section calls for all-wood doors, trim, window
trim, baseboard, kitchen cabinets, and counters for the condominiums,
shelving, paneling, and furnishing and installing finish hardware and
bathroom accessories.

Roofing and sheet metal   The flat roof is specified to be of four ply felt and hot pitch of the 20-year type but without bond. The sides of the mansard roof are specified to be covered with mineral-surfaced class C self-sealing 250-lb asphalt strip shingles, 5 in to the weather laid over heavy felt. All flashings are of copper-clad stainless steel. All caulking material is of urethane-epoxy.

Insulation   Thermal insulation is specified to be 4-in fiber glass with vapor barrier. Sound insulation is specified to be of blanket type in partitions between units and between units and public spaces.

Doors, windows, and glass   All sash and frames are specified to be of 0.062-in aluminum. Sash are double hung. Glass is federal specification-DD-G-451a.
 Doors are $1\frac{3}{4}$-in hollow metal and frames are of 16-gauge steel. Doors at fire walls are Underwriters-labeled with approved self-closing devices.

 Doors to shops are of wood.

 Office doors are solid core wood with steel frames.

 Stair doors are painted steel with steel frames.

 Lobby doors are aluminum glazed with safety glass.

 Doors through certain fire walls are rolling type with fusible links.

Partitions   Brick bearing walls separate the bays; interior partitions are of $\frac{1}{2}$-in gypsum board on steel studs with vinyl base; at corridors, two layers of $\frac{1}{2}$-in fire-code gypsum board and Thermafibre sound-attenuation blanket to studs; corridor and stairway partitions are of $\frac{5}{8}$-in fire-code gypsum board on metal studs with vinyl base.

Interior finishes   Residential condominium units are of vinyl wearing surface, 0.175 gauge, bonded to foam vinyl backing.
 General resilient floor tile is of $\frac{1}{8}$-in vinyl asbestos with molded-cove vinyl base.
 Other finishes are as indicated in Table 17-7.

Rubbish removal   A 24-in rubbish chute and a rubbish compactor are specified. The openings are of fire-resistant labeled metal, and a sprinkler head is placed over the top opening.

Elevators   The specification calls for two elevators of the worm-geared traction type with collective-selective control. Capacity 2000 lb and

TABLE 17-7   FINISH SPECIFICATIONS

Area	Floors	Party walls	Other walls	Ceilings
Offices	Tenant's choice	Sand-blasted brick	Painted gypsum board	Natural wood beams
Stores	Tenant's choice	Sand-blasted brick	Painted gypsum board	Natural wood beams
Corridors	Carpet ULB rated	. . . .	Painted gypsum board	Natural wood beams
Stairwells	Smooth concrete	. . . .	Painted gypsum board	
Basement	Tenant's choice or smooth concrete	Sand-blasted brick	Painted gypsum board	Natural wood beams

speed 200 ft/min. Each elevator has seven landings furnished with approved two-speed automatic doors.

Plumbing   A summary of the plumbing specifications follows:

City water, 6-in water service

Sewer is connected to existing city sewer pipe, 8 in at building to 12 in at street end. New storm sewer on south side of building, pipe 6 to 8 to 10 in; on north side of building pipe 8 to 12 to 18 in empties into city storm sewer. Copper gutters and downspouts empty into storm sewer. Piping for gas is black iron. Soil and waste is cast iron, part bell and spigot, part no hub. Approved standpipes in each stair hall.

Toilet rooms (basement): one men and one women, two units of each type of fixture.

Fixtures, Kohler & Kohler.

Two 2-in Weil sewage-ejector pumps handle first floor and basement. 6-in Weil sump pumps (50 gal/min) in three locations, one at each end and one in the middle; each has a standby.

HVAC   The heating is supplied by two Cleaver-Brooks oil-fired Scotch marine-type boilers. The fuel-oil storage tank is of 10,250-gal capacity, and no. 2 oil is used. Hot water is circulated to individual fan-coil units located throughout the building.

The cooling is supplied by two natural-gas-driven evaporative condenser units located in the basement.[1] The cold water is circulated to the individual fan-coil units.

[1]Original plans called for the boilers and chiller units to be on the roof, but units were found which by some adjustment would fit the existing basement headroom.

Individual exhaust fans are specified in every kitchen and in every toilet room whether residential or other. Ventilation is supplied to corridors and other space by roof fans. Cooling tower is located on the roof.

Hot water is supplied by two gas-fired Patterson-Kelly 40 gal/min heaters.

Sprinklers   A complete automatic wet sprinkler system throughout is specified, complete with sprinkler alarms as called for by code.

Electrical   The electrical systems are 120/208 V single phase three-wire and 120/208 V three-phase four-wire for lighting and power complete with breakers and panel boards. All branch circuit wiring is of Romex cable. Bus duct to connect to meter panel. All lighting is fluorescent. There is a 30-kW Onan emergency generator.

17-7   THE FINANCING

See Table 17-8.

The Statement of Estimated Income and Expense

The statements given in Tables 17-4 and 17-5, used to obtain the financing, are summarized in Table 17-9.

The Boston Waterfront Development Corp (BWDC) (the recycling group) was able to obtain interim financing based on the statements in Tables 17-8 and 17-9 from the Connecticut Bank and Trust Co. and the Builders Investment Group of Valley Forge, Pennsylvania (an REIT).

TABLE 17-8   TOTAL COST OF PROJECT

Acquisition cost*	$1,195,000
Granite Building:	
Construction cost	4,350,000
Indirect costs†	2,024,000
Pilot House:	
Construction cost	1,053,000
Indirect costs†	560,000
Total cost	$9,182,000
Less sales of residential condominiums	5,864,000
Remaining in property	$3,318,000
Recycling group equity	750,000

*Includes Granite Building (Parcel A), Pilot House (Parcel D), and Parcels B, C, E, and F.

†Includes architect's, engineer's, and other fees and interest during construction, etc.

TABLE 17-9 SUMMARIZED INCOME AND EXPENSES FOR GRANITE
BUILDING, PARKING LOT, AND PILOT HOUSE

Granite Building:		
Total EGI	$501,000	
Expenses (not including finance charges)	235,000	
Net income		$266,000
Parking lot:		
Total income	$105,000	
Expenses (not including finance charges)	55,300	
Net income		50,000
Pilot House:		
Total EGI	$311,500	
Expenses (not including finance charges)	122,600	
Net income		188,900
Total estimated net income before finance charges		$504,900

The permanent financing is by the Equitable Life Assurance Society of
the United States.

In addition to the financial details the lenders also carefully examined the marketing surveys, the neighborhood surveys, the rent comparisons, and the plans and specifications.

17-8 BIDDING AND THE CONSTRUCTION CONTRACT

The plans and specifications were developed by Carl Koch and Associates, Inc. The structural and overall mechanical engineering was done
by consulting engineering firms, and the actual detailed engineering
design, which was based on the standard set by the consultants, was
performed by the plumbing, HVAC, and electrical contractors, who
included the cost of the design in their contract prices.

The total cost of the construction contract was negotiated with the
Kirkland Construction Co., a local general contractor. It was a fixed
sum, and the form of contract was an AIA Form 101, Stipulated Sum.
The contract amount was for $5,403,000 and the general contractor, the
owner, and the architect had an agreement among them that no essential extras at any increased cost were to be considered unless there was
a compensating reduction in some other piece of construction that
might be considered an extra amenity but was nonessential.

The contract between the architect and owner was on AIA Form
B331, Professional Fee Plus Expenses.

17-9 MARKETING THE PROJECT

The original marketing efforts in behalf of the residential condominiums were made by Carl Koch by means of newspaper advertisements and by follow-up of telephone inquiries. There were also handsome rental brochures and signs on the construction project which could be seen by anyone approaching the waterfront. Later a full-time salesperson was employed to solicit prospective condominium purchasers. This was a highly successful effort based on convincing rent payers that this kind of condominium was much the better buy.

The office space was advertised, and there were telephone surveys of smaller users who might like to get out of the downtown area and gain some individuality by occupying space in a project of this kind. To attract the first tenants the space was offered at a lower rate than that for downtown space.

The shops were rented through advertising that was slanted toward the boutique type of tenant or the "different" kind of restaurant which would flourish in a historic waterfront location of this kind.

One restaurant is already doing very well. The neighborhood is not yet fully developed, but when it is, it should attract heavy traffic of downtown office-building workers and tourists.

17-10 MANAGEMENT

The construction project manager, James Craig, took over the interim management of the project as it was ready for occupancy. His other duties, however, prevented him from giving it his full time, and in early 1975 a professional management firm, Ryan, Elliott and Coughlin Management Corp., took over the almost completed project and appointed Alden Gifford, a professional manager, as project manager.

It is interesting to note after almost 2 years of partial occupancy, extraordinary expense, and repayment of old accounts that Ryan, Elliott and Coughlin have produced a statement of projected income and expense for the first full year of normal operation (Table 17-10).

17-11 CONCLUSION

This project has been in progress since 1966, and a part of it is not yet completed. One parcel which is to be a restaurant is in negotiation. The parking lot has not been fully developed. The project has taken a great

TABLE 17-10   PROJECTED POTENTIAL INCOME AND EXPENSE
STATEMENT*

Gross income:		
Pilot House	$298,500	
Granite Building, Retail stores	227,500	
Offices	265,500	
Basement	18,500	
Proposed restaurant	28,000	
Marina	18,200	
Parking	150,100	
Miscellaneous	2,000	
Overages on percentage rentals	25,000	
Tax clauses and escalation	47,000	
		$1,080,000
Operating expenses:		
Insurance	23,000	
Electric	26,000	
Gas	24,000	
Staff	40,000	
Payroll taxes	6,500	
Employee benefits	5,000	
Repairs and maintenance	18,000	
Air conditioning contract and repairs	3,200	
Elevator contract and repairs	1,500	
Supplies	10,000	
Cleaning	24,000	
Snow removal	1,000	
Pest control	1,500	
Rubbish removal	5,000	
Project security	1,200	
Water	1,000	
Legal	10,000	
Accounting	4,000	
Management	18,000	
Office expenses	2,200	
Miscellaneous	500	
		$225,000
Real estate taxes	281,000	
Mortgage interest:		
Equitable	$378,000	
BIG (construction loan)	3,600	
		381,600
Total expense		$887,600
Estimated cash flow		$192,400

*Based on 1 year partial and 1 year full management and on complete development.

deal of the architect's time and that of the construction manager. The final estimated cash flow when the entire project is in operation is conservatively estimated at $192,000 on an equity of $750,000. The rate of return is better than 25 percent, and accelerated depreciation will make this practically net income.

18

CASE STUDY TWO:
RECYCLING A WAREHOUSE
INTO AN OFFICE BUILDING,
DARIEN, CONNECTICUT

18-1 HOW THE PROJECT WAS STARTED

A number of years before this project was conceived, a large distribution and home-delivery service company built a warehouse distribution center in a business zone of Darien, Connecticut. As time went on, this 15,000-ft² building became too small for the purpose and was superseded by a larger building in another town. The building, which is on leased land, was therefore left idle with no specific ideas of what could be done with it. The building is located close to a neighborhood shopping center and adjacent to the Noroton Heights Station of Conrail. Thousands of commuters walked or drove within 100 yd of it, but no one had the imagination to do anything about it.

Gary Silcox is in the real estate business. He kept seeing this apparently structurally sound building lying idle and thought that some use should be found for it. He spoke to a local commercial real estate broker, who found that the building could be purchased and that the land lease had 90 years still to go. It started to look like the beginning of a deal.

Before the purchase could be consummated, however, many things had to be done. Silcox, who is the managing partner of a real estate consortium named Echo Six, entered into an agreement with the owners of the building under which he had the option to purchase if he accomplished certain steps at certain times. As each step was accomplished, he was given additional time to complete the next step. These investigations were for the benefit of both the seller and the buyer and there was no penalty if the sale was not consummated.

18-2   THE FEASIBILITY STUDY

Not in order of their importance the steps to be taken were as follows:

A marketing survey to determine the best and highest use for the building.

Preliminary plans and specifications to show how the building was to be altered.

A letter of intent from a mortgage lender, satisfactory to the owner, to show how the purchase and the alteration were to be financed. In order to obtain such a letter of intent it was of course necessary for the entrepreneur to prepare a financial statement which included the cost of the proposed recycling.

18-3   THE MARKETING SURVEY

Darien is a prosperous community located in Fairfield County in southwestern Connecticut. The town has a population of 20,000 and is known as a "bedroom" town. It is 40 mi from New York City and is located on the main line of Conrail. The town is in the so-called megalopolis, i.e., the corridor in the northeast connecting Washington, D.C., New York City, and Boston. This corridor contains the highest concentration of population, business, banking, and the arts in the United States and probably the world.

There has been very little business and no industry in the town. Heretofore the majority of the wage earners have been commuting to New York City, which is 1 hour by train, but this pattern is changing as more and more business is locating out of the metropolitan center to the suburbs.

Darien is very strictly zoned for single-family dwellings. The zoning regulations also provide for retail business, service business, small office buildings, and for designed office and research centers. Since these areas are quite small compared with the total area of the town, not much land is available for new office buildings.

The past several years have seen an influx of large corporate headquarters into southwestern Connecticut. Such corporate giants as Xerox, Continental Can, American Can, Combustion Engineering, Chesebrough Pond, Avco, and General Telephone and Electronics have moved to Greenwich, Stamford, and Norwalk, all of which are located within a 10-mi radius of Darien. With them these corporations have brought a host of smaller satellite companies who do not require entire buildings but need from 5000 to 30,000 or more ft^2 as office space. These smaller companies, like the large ones, are attracted by the younger female labor force which is available here but which will not travel to the metropolis because of the time and expense involved and the dangers of the inner cities. The survey showed that there was a strong market for office space in southwestern Connecticut.

Transportation

One of the basic considerations in office location is transportation (Fig. 18-1). Darien is on the main line of Conrail, which provides through service to New York, Boston, and Washington, D.C. It is on the Con-

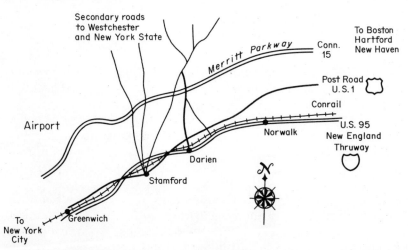

FIGURE 18-1   Darien is located on a major throughway only 3 mi from another major parkway. It is on the main line of Conrail (Boston–New York–Washington, D.C.).

necticut Turnpike, an all-purpose throughway, and Greenwich, Norwalk, Stamford, or Bridgeport are all less than ½ h away. La Guardia Airport and Kennedy International Airport are less than 1 h by automobile. Private planes can take off from Armonk and Bridgeport, which are less than ½ h away. Darien lies at the terminus of a state road that taps central Westchester and northern Fairfield counties. It is accessible to the workers and within 1 h of a transportation center to the entire world. Any kind of business office can locate here.

Local Amenities

Owners of office space or employers of office help know that certain conveniences should be available to the employees within short walking distance in the city or short driving distance in the suburban areas. In this instance the building is immediately adjacent to a supermarket and to other shops. There are several restaurants not more than 5 min drive away. There are also boutiques, men's shops, a library, and other amenities within very short driving distance. The building is across the street from a railroad station and adjacent to a throughway and to roads leading to towns in Westchester and Connecticut. The general atmosphere is conducive to good employee relations.

18-4   ZONING AND BUILDING REQUIREMENTS

According to the zoning map of Darien, the building is located in a PB (planned retail business) zone. This zone allows retail business, professional and business offices, restaurants, etc., but no storage of motor vehicles, etc., except for daily parking space.

This zone is restrictive in order to allow for a good office-building atmosphere. The mininum lot size is 1 acre, and neither lot frontage nor depth can be less than 150 ft. A building cannot exceed 2½ stories or 30 ft in height and cannot cover more than 20 percent of the lot area. This would only allow a sort of "garden type" office building, which is very attractive to many prospective users.

The building in existence had been approved, and as the new use was not to exceed any of the set parameters (size, height, lot size, frontage, etc.), it was comparatively simple to obtain a preliminary opinion from the planning and zoning board that the proposed recycling and the new use would meet with no difficulty.

The Town of Darien operates under the State of Connecticut Building Code, which is patterned to a great extent on the BOCA Code.

18-5 THE FORMATION OF THE TEAM AND THE INPUT

It was now time to employ an architect-engineer to draw preliminary and eventually final working drawings; to obtain zoning and building department approvals; to make a detailed survey of the existing building; to employ an experienced business-oriented real estate broker; and to come up with a final decision what to build and how to build it. From these inputs a financial statement would be prepared which would contain sufficient detailed information to induce a lender to commit himself to financing the project.

The Architect-Engineer

Silcox interviewed a number of local architects and chose David Bruce Falconer, AIA, of Darien, for the quality of his existing work, the quality of his ideas for the proposed recycling, and because of his knowledge of local codes, working conditions, and town officialdom. His contract was for a fixed fee (AIA Form B141) with provisions for additional payment for work over and above the original concept. The first step was a thorough inspection of the existing building in order to determine how it could be structurally altered at the least expense and with the smallest waste of rentable space.

THE SURVEY OF THE EXISTING BUILDING

The building as it existed was 142 ft long by 105 ft wide, which with an entrance vestibule came to 15,000 ft². The lot size is 255 ft wide by 293 ft deep plus an access road. The first floor was a 5-in-thick reinforced concrete slab over a minimum of 8 in of bank-run gravel. The roof was supported by 6-ft-deep girders, which rested on steel columns and provided a clear span over the entire width (105 ft). The clear height from the top of the concrete slab to the underside of the girders was 15 ft 11 in. The exterior was of brick and 8-in concrete block. The footings were examined and found to be sound. The fenestration and openings for doors were minimal except for clerestory windows at the top of the two side elevations. The plumbing, mechanical, and electrical installations had been planned for very few resident employees and were minimal. The roof was in poor shape and required replacement.

The Real Estate Broker-Consultant

The real estate expert recommended strongly that the new use be for an office building. There was a need for office space in the entire area. He could produce several substantial business concerns that were willing to enter into negotiations for office space and who could use anywhere from one-half a floor (7500 ft²) to the entire building, which could be 30,000 ft² if a second floor were to be added. This recommendation was accepted.

18-6   THE DECISION

It was to be an office building. The clear inside height of 15 ft 11 in was too high for one story and not enough for two stories. The answer was to eliminate the deep girders and substitute a light steel interior structure that would support a second floor and a new roof structure. This would give an inside clear height of over 21 ft. The fenestration was almost nonexistent. An office building requires windows, but not too large ones because of energy wastage. The bare-brick exterior walls were to be refurbished to add architectural interest and quality. Entirely new mechanical, plumbing, and electrical systems had to be installed. It was to be like building a new building inside of an existing one. The architect-engineer drew preliminary plans and outline specifications sufficient for fairly close preliminary estimating.

The entrepreneur managed to find a tenant who was willing to sign a master lease for the entire 30,000 ft². The tenant was a company of national reputation, and the lease was subject to final negotiations on term, rental rate, and date of occupancy. Sufficient parameters were spelled out to prevent the lease from being nebulous.

A preliminary financial statement was prepared for the financial institution which had shown interest in the preliminary enquiries. The financial statement looked somewhat as shown in Table 18-1. With this statement the prospective owners and recyclers included preliminary plans and specifications, a master lease with a well-known company, a preliminary construction contract, an indication from the Town of Darien that the proposed recycling would conform with zoning and building codes, and a copy of the agreement with the present owner and a copy of the land lease.

18-7   THE FINANCING

Based on the information received and on the reputation of the applicants, a permanent mortgage commitment was given by the Society for Savings of Hartford, at 9½ percent for 27 years. It was to be effective as of the completion of construction. This commitment for a take-out mortgage was taken to the Union Trust Co., which maintains a branch

TABLE 18-1 PRELIMINARY FINANCIAL STATEMENT FOR ALTERATION
OF WAREHOUSE TO OFFICE BUILDING

72 Heights Rd., Noroton (Darien), Conn.
New owners (Under contract of sale): Echo Six, Gary Silcox, managing partner

Cost:		
Cost of property as is, subject to land lease*	$ 225,000	
Preliminary negotiated construction contract per attached plans and specifications	650,000	
Architect, legal, and administrative expenses†	130,000	
Interest during construction	35,000	
Total	$1,040,000	
Income and expense:		
Annual income		$300,000
Annual operating expense including taxes, maintenance, fuel, electricity, etc.	$ 120,000	
Real estate commissions	18,000	138,000
Remaining for mortgage interest, amortization, and return on investment		$162,000

*90 years remaining of 99-year lease.
†All preliminary costs for investigation of market, feasibility, etc., borne by owner.

in Darien. This bank consented to furnish the construction loan. The
terms were 10 percent plus 1 point at the start. Both commitments were
for $1 million.

18-8 FINAL PLANS AND SPECIFICATIONS

With the financing secure it was now possible to proceed with complete working drawings and specifications preparatory to obtaining
zoning-board approval and a building permit and then to the obtaining
of firm bids.

The work consisted of the alteration of a single-story open warehouse structure into a two-story office building while keeping the
original shell of the structure except for cutting new openings and
refurbishing the exterior (Fig. 18-2).

Structural Steel

The existing steel columns, which were on 24-ft centers around the
perimeter of the building and which supported the 6-ft clear-span
girders across the entire width of 105 ft, were retained. The new second
floor is supported by steel columns on 20- by 20-ft centers, except for
the center bays, which are 20 by 22 ft. The girders between the new

FIGURE 18-2   Exterior of remodeled warehouse.

columns support open-web steel joists on 3-ft centers. The two lines of columns at the center bays go through the second floor up to the underside of the roof and support the roof structure (see Fig. 18-3). This consists of 2-ft-deep girders plus 8-in purlins instead of the 6-ft girders, which were removed. The roof is supported on open-web steel joists, which are 1 ft 8 in deep and rest on the purlins. The total depth of the roof structure is now 3 ft instead of 6 ft (Fig. 18-3). The new window and door openings are supported by steel lintels.

Floors

The first floor is of 2½ in of concrete poured over 15-lb felt vapor barrier. This concrete is superimposed over the existing 5-in concrete slab. The second floor is of 3 in of concrete poured over a metal deck. The decking is specified to be phosphate-coated with baked-on enamel finish.

Foundations and Site Work

The only foundations that were necessary were the footings for the new columns. The initial inspection of the property showed that the original foundations were in excellent condition. They consisted of spread footings down to 3-ton soil and heavy-concrete grade beams to support the exterior walls.

The sitework consisted of the necessary fill and blacktop for the additional parking required by the zoning regulations. Ditching, pip-

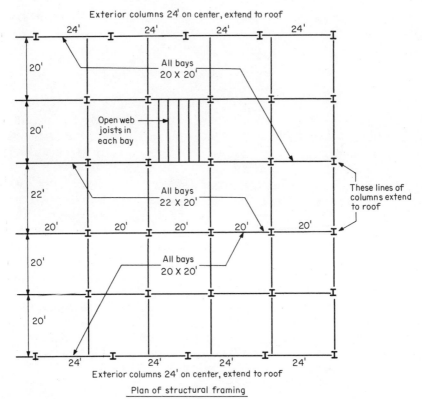

Exterior columns 24' on center, extend to roof

All bays
20 X 20'

Open web
joists in
each bay

All bays
22 X 20'

These lines of
columns extend
to roof

All bays
20 X 20'

Exterior columns 24' on center, extend to roof

Plan of structural framing

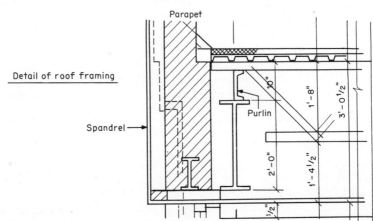

Detail of roof framing

Parapet

Purlin

Spandrel

10"

1'-8"

3'-0½"

2'-0"

1'-4½"

½"

FIGURE 18-3

ing, and manholes were also required for new sanitary sewer, water, and electrical lines and for storm drainage. New low-level lighting and certain planting in accord with the regulations also had to be installed.

Masonry

The existing building had only two large openings for trucks and a small pedestrian entrance on the first floor and a line of fixed clerestory windows on the two longer elevations. These had to be completely changed to meet the requirements of a modern office building.

Openings had to be cut for new windows, exit doors, and the main entrance. There are 41 window openings and 4 new door openings. The clerestory strip windows were removed, and those openings plus the existing door openings were closed. All the new door and window openings were patched with matching brick for the returns and with brick sills. The rear of the building is close to the public road, and the new owners were obligated by the Town to build a brick facing over the existing exposed concrete-block wall.

The spandrels above the head of the first- and second-floor windows are of exposed aggregate set in a colored matrix, which gives some architectural character to the exterior.

Stairs and Exits

In accordance with building-code requirements the stairways are of steel with cement treads, and each one leads to an exit to grade. There are two stairways which are enclosed in 2-h firewalls plus an open main-entrance stairway, which is decorative and in an open vestibule.

Doors, Windows, and Glass

The fire doors are self-closing hollow-metal Underwriters-labeled. The entrance doors are of aluminum with concealed floor checks. All door frames are of pressed steel, and all core doors are of $1\frac{3}{4}$-in hollow metal. The architect specified all partition doors to be $1\frac{3}{4}$-in hollow-core wood doors in steel bucks.

The windows are of heavy-gauge Duranodic aluminum of the sliding type. They are all double-glazed. The aluminum is finished with acrylic enamel over a chromate sprayed-on coating.

Roofing, Sheet Metal, and Insulation

The roof is of four-ply, 20-year-bonded type, using tarred felts and tar pitch surfaced with gravel. Base flashing is the same as the roof, and cap flashing is stainless steel. The roof insulation is of 2 in of rigid foam blocks laid in hot pitch over a metal deck. The flashing is of copper-reinforced fabric or annealed soft stainless steel.

Exterior-wall insulation is of 1- by 24-in styrofoam, except behind the spandrels, where it is of 4-in minimum glass-wool batts.

Finishes

DRY WALL

The exterior walls are furred with ½-in gypsum board over metal furring. The architect specified the interior tenant partitions to be of ½-in gypsum board on each side of steel studs and in some cases specified a double layer of ½-in gypsum board on each side.

INTERIOR MASONRY

The men's and women's toilet rooms are enclosed in walls consisting of 4-in concrete block, a 2-in cavity, and 6-in concrete block covered with gypsum board. They are immediately adjacent to workspace (there is no central core) and had to be made completely soundproof.

ACOUSTICAL CEILINGS

The acoustical hung ceilings are of fissured mineral lay-in panels supported by an exposed-tee fire-rated grid. The panels are 24 by 48 in.

Floors

Floors in the tenant space were left as bare concrete to await tenants' requirements. The vestibule and toilet floors are of ceramic tile.

Electrical

Because of the minimal installation in the original structure the building needed an entirely new electrical installation from a new service line, transformer station, and switch gear to individual circuit wiring. An outline of the specification follows:

Complete underground electric service, including transformer compartment, conduits, metering, and wiring to meet utility-company standards

Main service switch and main distribution panel

Circuit-breaker panels for light and power

Lighting fixtures and lamps (24 in by 48 in, four-lamp fluorescents, flush-set with plastic lenses)

Incandescent fixtures as shown

All wiring devices, switches, boxes, conduits, etc.

Raceway system for outlets and lamp connections

Fire-alarm system activated by smoke detectors or by manual control

Plumbing

The original plumbing system was reconditioned almost in its entirety. There is a women's and men's toilet room on each of the two floors according to code.

The water piping is of copper and the sanitary piping of cast iron. There are connections for a drinking fountain, and there is a hot-water heater located in a first-floor utility room. All hot- and cold-water piping is insulated.

Heating, Ventilating, and Air Conditioning

Heating and cooling are provided by fan-coil units located on the exterior walls and by an interior duct system with anemostats located 26 ft from the perimeter.

The chiller, the cast-iron sectional boiler, and the pumps are located in a fireproofed first-floor mechanical room. The air-handling units are located on each floor adjacent to the toilet rooms and are ceiling-hung. The air-cooled condenser unit is on the roof.

All the duct work is insulated.

General

The plans and specifications call for an above-average office building. The walls and the roof are insulated, the hot- and cold-water lines and the air ducts are insulated. The windows are double-glazed. The interior finishes are of excellent quality (Fig. 18-4). The electrical, plumb-

FIGURE 18-4

ing, and HVAC systems are above average. The additional cost, which was minimal compared with the total cost, was more than justified by the quality of the tenants this building subsequently attracted.

18-9 BIDDING AND THE CONSTRUCTION CONTRACT

When the final plans and specifications were completed, the architect went out for bid. The bid form called for a base lump-sum bid plus prices for alternates. It also listed a number of items for which unit prices were requested. The bid sheet also requested a breakdown of prices with the general construction as one item and electrical, plumbing, and HVAC as separate items.

Bids were received, and the contract was given to the low bidder, Dryden, Inc., of Columbus, Ohio. The contract was for $650,000 and was prepared on the AIA Form A101, Standard Form of Agreement between Owner and Contractor, Stipulated Sum.

18-10 MARKETING THE PROJECT

As soon as financing was assured, Silcox, the principal of the recycling, started his marketing effort. Brochures were printed and sent to a number of commercial brokers in the entire metropolitan area. Advertisements were placed in *The New York Times* and *The Wall Street Journal.* Silcox interviewed the decision-making principals of many companies located in the metropolitan area. At the same time final negotiations were entered into with the signer of the original master lease.

The result of this intensive sales effort was to produce at least five serious offers to rent. Negotiations were carried on with all the prospects with preference being given to full-floor or entire-building renters. The first of the negotiations to produce a firm offer and a meeting of the minds determined the selection of the tenant, which is a nationwide company of impeccable financial standing and reputation.

The Lease

The lease is for 10 years at $10 per gross foot for the entire building or a total annual rent of $300,000. The tenant was granted a lump-sum amount of $45,000 for tenant-change work which was to be under the supervision of the architect. The owner was to provide all services.

18-11   MANAGEMENT

Management of the building is by the owner, who provides the following services:

Cleaning office space, stairways, toilets, and public corridors in accordance with a limited schedule. The tenant pays for any service over and above the schedule.

Electricity for HVAC, lighting, and power.

Maintenance and repairs to all building equipment, including ducts, dampers, thermostats, air-conditioning equipment, plumbing, etc.

Water and sewer charges.

Real estate taxes.

The lease contains an escalator clause based on taxes and operating costs over a base year.

18-12   CONCLUSION

This project is an excellent example of what can be done. An abandoned warehouse has become a first-rate 100 percent rented office building. It required imagination and ingenuity on the part of the owner and the architect, and the broker-consultant helped. The return on the investment is very high and thanks to accelerated depreciation the income is tax-free for the next 6 to 7 years. To reiterate, recycling can be extremely rewarding.

19

CASE STUDY THREE:
THE IRONFRONTS,
RICHMOND, VIRGINIA

19-1 HOW THIS PROJECT ORIGINATED

The recycling of the four ironfront buildings on East Main Street in
Richmond, Virginia came about almost by chance. Until a few years
ago there were several more of these buildings in the row, but East
Main Street has become a preferred location for new office buildings,
and to make room for one, several ironfront buildings to the east of the
subject were demolished. The resultant outcry of historically and architecturally minded Richmonders put an end to any further thoughts of
demolishing any more of these buildings. The buildings were underutilized and almost derelict (Fig. 19-1). They were in private hands, and
they were being taxed. The taxes plus even minimum maintenance
could not be justified by the rentals, and something had to be done.

The only hope for increased income was to recycle the buildings to
attract tenants who would be willing to pay rentals comparable to
downtown office-building rates. The first step was to employ an architect. The firm of Glave, Newman and Anderson was chosen to make a

FIGURE 19-1   The ironfront buildings before recycling.

survey of the buildings to see what could be done and to estimate what it might cost to perform a major renovation.

The study was made. There was a thorough inspection of the physical condition of the existing structure and line drawings of what could be done to make the buildings attractive to prospective tenants. Then the project came to a standstill. The owners seemed unwilling to spend the sizable amount of money necessary to bring the plans, the survey, the construction, and income and expense estimates, etc., to the point where a financial institution could be approached for funding. At this point the architects offered to invest their fee in the project and to become partners in the venture. From this time on the recycling became a reality.

It should be noted that in many recyclings the architect has taken a leading role. He has the imagination and the structural know-how to be able to see how a silk purse can be made of a sow's ear. After their initial survey Glave, Newman and Anderson could foresee what the end product would be and were willing to invest their sizable fee in it.

19-2   THE MARKETING SURVEY: THE AREA AND THE CITY

Before a great amount of time and money is spent on any major recycling and before the final use of such a recycling is determined, it is essential for the entrepreneur to become aware of the economic background of the area and the economic trend of the particular neighborhood. Such data can be obtained from chambers of commerce, neighborhood business associations, census reports, redevelopment authorities, local real estate brokers, banks, business magazines and so forth.

The Area

Richmond, besides being the capital of Virginia, is also the industrial and financial center of the state. Over 53,000 persons are employed in manufacturing in the Richmond metropolitan area, which encompasses the city of Richmond and Henrico, Chesterfield, and Hanover counties. The area has leading manufacturing facilities in tobacco, chemicals, aluminum, and paper industries, with major plants for pharmaceuticals, paints, fertilizers, food, metal fabrication, and clothing.

Phillip Morris has constructed a new $100 million manufacturing and research complex some 6 mi south of the city. The Reynolds Metals Company has its headquarters 6 mi west of the city. The A. H. Robins Company, a leading pharmaceutical producer, is located some 2.5 mi northwest of downtown Richmond. Other major firms located within a few miles' radius of the downtown area are the Ethyl Corporation, Robertshaw Controls Company, Virginia-Carolina Corporation, Commonwealth Natural Gas Corporation, and A.M.F. Company.

The City

Richmond occupies a pivotal position in Virginia's urban corridor between the port area of Hampton Roads (Norfolk and Newport News), approximately 100 mi southeast, and Washington, D.C., approximately 100 mi to the north.

The Richmond area population has been growing at a rate about equal to that of the state in general (Table 19-1). There is every indication that this growth trend will continue into the foreseeable future. The rate of increase has been slowing down noticeably, however. This is a local indication that the national trend toward zero population

TABLE 19-1 POPULATION (in thousands of people)

	1960	1970	1975 est.	Change, % 1960–70	Change, % 1970–75
City of Richmond	219	249	233	+14	−6
Richmond metropolitan area	436	518	547	+19	+6
Commonwealth of Virginia	3954	4650	4927	+18	+6

growth is starting to take hold in the metropolitan area, as well as the effects of a constantly growing base upon which the rate of increase must be computed.

The Economy

Thanks to its location, Richmond has long been a center of commerce, finance, trade, and manufacturing. It is the headquarters city for the Fifth District Federal Reserve Bank and three of Virginia's five largest commercial banks, as well as 34 insurance companies, the major tobacco companies, Reynolds Metals Company, and The Seaboard Coastline Railroad, and is the regional headquarters for a large number of national companies. Richmond has over 850 wholesale distributors and over 580 manufacturing plants. Major employers are shown in Table 19-2.

The general employment picture in the metropolitan Richmond economy is one of broadly based and well-diversified growth. Increasing at a rate higher than the state in general, this growth in employment underscores the continued expansion of the area's economic base. Also, the diversity and growth of employment in the Richmond area have served to insulate against unemployment during downturns in the business cycle. The approximate percentage distribution of employment for the Richmond metropolitan area in 1975 is given in Table 19-3.

Throughout the period from 1967 to 1975 the rate of unemployment in the Richmond area has been consistently below both state and national levels by substantial margins. During the recent recession, the Richmond area unemployment rate has averaged a good point or more below the national average. In May 1976, the Richmond standard metropolitan statistical area unemployment rate was 3.7 percent, while the state rate was 5.0 percent and the national rate was 6.7 percent.

TABLE 19-2   MAJOR EMPLOYERS IN THE RICHMOND METROPOLITAN AREA

	Estimated number of employees
State and local government	50,000
Federal government	8,000
Medical College of Virginia	6,500
Phillip Morris, Inc.	7,000
American Tobacco Co.	2,000
E. I. Du Pont	4,500
Reynolds Metals	4,500

TABLE 19-3 PERCENTAGE DISTRIBUTION OF EMPLOYMENT IN
RICHMOND METROPOLITAN AREA

Manufacturing	18.4
Local and state government	18.7
Retail trade	15.6
Services	16.8
Finances, real estate, insurance	8.2
Wholesale	7.0
Communications, transportation	6.5
Construction	5.5
Federal government	3.0
Other	0.3
	100.0

INCOME

The per household effective buying income for the Richmond metropolitan area was $14,858 in 1974, compared with $13,944 for the state
and $13,722 for the country. The metropolitan area has shown a 39.3
percent increase in per household effective buying income since 1969,
and this compares favorably with increases of 43.7 and 36.6 percent by
the state and the country, respectively, for the same period. However,
the metropolitan area's ranking in the country dropped from sixty-
ninth position in 1969 to seventy-third in 1974.

We conclude that while the Richmond metropolitan area has
dropped in national ranking in the majority of economic categories in
the past 5 years, the area has shown a steady increase in each category,
indicating a positive growth pattern.

RETAIL SALES

The per household total retail sales showed a dramatic increase from
1969 to 1974, both in the city and the metropolitan area. The per
household total retail sales of $10,985 for 1974 for Richmond is an
increase of 23.8 percent over 1969. The metropolitan area in 1969 had a
per household total retail sales figure of $5939, with a national ranking
of one hundred first in the country. 1974 shows retail sales per household of $9169 and a fifty-seventh place ranking in the country. While
the metropolitan area's national ranking in population and number of
households has decreased, the per household total retail sales ranking
has increased significantly, indicating that more people are spending at
a faster rate than in the past 5 years.

Transportation

HIGHWAY

Good north-south and east-west interstate highway connections are easily accessible in Richmond. I-95 (north-south) and I-64 (east-west) intersect near the downtown area. I-95 provides good access to the entire east coast, and I-64 runs from the Tidewater area of Virginia, to the east, to the western part of the state. Two circumferential routes proposed for the future, I-295 on the north and east and Virginia 288 on the south and west, are planned to join south and west of Richmond, encircling the city. Construction is planned to begin during 1978 with completion during 1981.

Richmond is served by four railroads: the C & O; Richmond, Fredericksburg and Potomac; Southern; and Seaboard Coast Line. It also has good commercial airline service, with regularly scheduled flights by Altair, Davenport, Eastern, Piedmont, and United Air Lines via Richard E. Byrd International Airport in Henrico County. The James River is navigable from Hampton Roads on the Chesapeake Bay via a 35-ft deep channel for ships serving Richmond's deepwater terminal. The terminal has berths for two vessels.

Richmond is an economically stable city of consistent growth. It has been relatively free of major economic recessions, labor problems, etc. In the appraisers' opinion, it is a viable area for real estate investment and will maintain such viability for the foreseeable future.

19-3   THE MARKETING SURVEY: THE NEIGHBORHOOD

The property is located on East Main Street east of 10th Street. This location is in the heart of the downtown business and financial district and is within walking distance of finance and business, government, and the medical center.

Finance and Business

The two largest banks in the state are within two blocks on Main Street. Numerous banks, savings and loan associations, insurance companies, stock brokers, and real estate firms are located along Main Street between 4th and 11th Streets.

The new Federal Reserve District headquarters is under construction three blocks south of the subject.

Government

Capitol Square is one block west and one block north of subject at 9th and Bank Streets. In this square is located the Virginia State Capitol, the finance building, and state office buildings. On Capitol Street are the State Library and Supreme Court of Appeals. The Virginia Employment Commission building is one block west of the subject at 7th and Main Streets.

The Richmond City Hall is located on Broad Street (4 1/2 blocks from subject).

The Federal Building, located just north of City Hall, was completed in 1962. A federal courts building is presently under construction in this area. The Central Post Office and federal courts buildings are two blocks east of subject on Main Street.

Medical Center

The six-block complex constituting the Medical College of Virginia Medical Center is seven blocks north of subject.

19-4   SURVEY OF THE BUILDING

Before the architect and engineer could start their final design for the recycling, a detailed survey of the building was made. The buildings have basements which are 10 ft 9 in below Main Street and subbasements which are 9 ft 3 in below the basement but only 5 ft below the rear alley. The basements are dry. Some of the brick piers and foundation walls showed signs of deterioration, but, since it was not serious, they could be repaired rather than replaced. The foundations themselves were sound. A new concrete floor slab was necessary in two of the buildings.

The buildings are separated by 18 in brick party walls, which are in excellent condition. Openings would have to be cut through these walls so that all space in the four buildings would be accessible from a central elevator and stairways.

The basement and first floor structural floors consisted of 3 by 12 joists laid over a center beam supported on 12 by 12 in masonry piers. The upper floors were of 3 by 12 joists 16 in on center spanning the entire clear width of each building. It was found that some of this structure would have to be replaced, especially in the basement and first floor.

The stairways and means of egress did not conform to present code and would have to be replaced with fireproof stairs enclosed in legal fire walls. All the floors would have to be framed for the stair wells and for two new elevators.

All waterproofing and caulking, including the entire roof, would have to be replaced, including a bulkhead for a stairway.

Exterior windows and frames would have to be repaired or replaced where beyond repair. The iron front itself required some replacement of broken parts and complete refurbishing.

The plumbing, heating, ventilating, and electrical systems had deteriorated to the point where it was best to remove them almost completely and replace them with new systems conforming to code.

To summarize, the architect could start with a structure that had no groundwater problems, sound foundations, sound masonry, and a generally sound structural frame. It was a viable shell.

19-5   ZONING AND BUILDING CODES

Zoning

The project is located in a B4 central business district. Following are the requirements and limitations of the code:

Yards.   No front yard; no side yard except adjacent to dwelling uses. No rear yard except adjacent to dwelling uses

Land-use intensity.   Floor-area ratio not to exceed 6.0

Height.   No maximum-height limitation except as set by an inclined plane from center of abutting street and rising at an angle of 1 ft horizontal to 4 ft vertical, 75° from horizontal

Building Code

Richmond has adopted the BOCA code as its official building code, and the building was designed under this code. The architects had also to file a statement with the Virginia Air Pollution Control Board, as follows: "The buildings will contain less than 249,000 ft^2 and will be occupied by fewer than 900 employees. The buildings will be electrically heated. There will be no incinerator. There will be no demolition of asbestos-bearing material." A somewhat similar statement was filed with the city water and sewer departments.

GENERAL REQUIREMENTS OF THE CODE

Under the code this structure is in use group B, which pertains to office buildings used for the transaction of business and the rendering of professional services.

Construction   The construction classification in this case is 3A, which refers to a building with masonry bearing walls and of heavy-timber construction. The fire-resistant rating is obtained by protecting the partitions, structural elements, floors, ceiling, roof, and exitways with approved noncombustible material which meets the specified code standards.

The 3A classification under which the buildings were recycled specifies 2-h exterior walls, 2-h interior bearing walls, party walls, shafts, and stairway walls and specified sizes for framing and floor construction.

Area and height limitations   Under use B and construction classification 3A the buildings are limited to five stories or 65 ft (these buildings are only four stories). The area for floor is limited to 21,600 ft². It was intended that the four buildings involved in the project be used as a single building and by cutting openings in the existing party walls each floor is used horizontally. The total area per floor is less than the prescribed limit.

Means of egress   The code allows a maximum occupancy of 100 ft² per person and a minimum of two fireproof exitways. The maximum allowable distance to an exitway is 200 ft in a building without a fire-suppression system and 300 ft with such a system. As these buildings were to be sprinklered, the 300-ft distance was allowable.

OSHA Requirements

The Occupational Safety and Health Act (OSHA) of 1970 adds another dimension to the various precautions which are usually taken by a good construction contractor to promote safety on the job. It is generally thought that the commission which promulgated and enforces this act is somewhat overzealous and causes extra expense for the contractor. In this particular instance the budget allows $6000 for complying with OSHA regulations in addition to the normally budgeted sums for temporary protection, barricades, scaffolding, fire protection, and other temporary services. The architect or developer who proposes to engage in recycling work should remember, however, that this kind of work is more hazardous than normal construction. In normal construction the worker is aware that there are holes for pipe shafts, stairwells, and elevator shafts and that certain work follows in a regular sequence. In recycling there are holes where stairways or mechanical equipment have been removed; there is demolition and repair work on masonry, floors, ceilings, etc.; i.e., there is constantly unexpected danger to the worker. In such instances the OSHA strict regulations certainly justify themselves, and extra money should be budgeted to comply with them.

Energy Conservation

The 1976 Supplement of the BOCA Code (the code under which Richmond operates) under its section on energy conservation regulates the design and construction of the exterior envelopes of buildings and the design and selection of HVAC, water-heating, electrical distribution and illumination, and any other energy-using equipment. Many cities and states are now engaged in adding such a section to their codes. It will not be long before the architect and the engineer will be forced to design buildings to meet code or ASHRAE[1] energy-conservation standards before a building permit can be obtained. The architect's design requirements are spelled out in detail, whereas the engineer's design parameters, because they are so complicated, simply refer to the ASHRAE standards.

The architect's design to comply with these regulations is shown in Figs. 19-2 to 19-4.

19-6   HOW THE DECISION WAS MADE

Because of the location and the layout of the buildings it was inevitable that they would have to be converted into office use. Because of the location on a street extensively used by office employees, it was almost a foregone conclusion that there should be retail stores and that there should be a restaurant accessible from the street. The basement could be used for shops and service facilities and the subbasement for heavy service facilities or repair shops or light assembly work. But while the final use was thus established, it was by no means certain that it would pay and it was not certain what the level of the recycling should be. For this determination the architect assembled a team.

The Architect-Engineer

Older buildings which retain the exterior architectural character of the period in which they were built seem to attract tenants looking for individuality in their housing or office space. The challenge to the

---

[1]American Society of Heating, Refrigerating and Air-Conditioning Engineers, 345 E. 47 St., New York NY 10017.

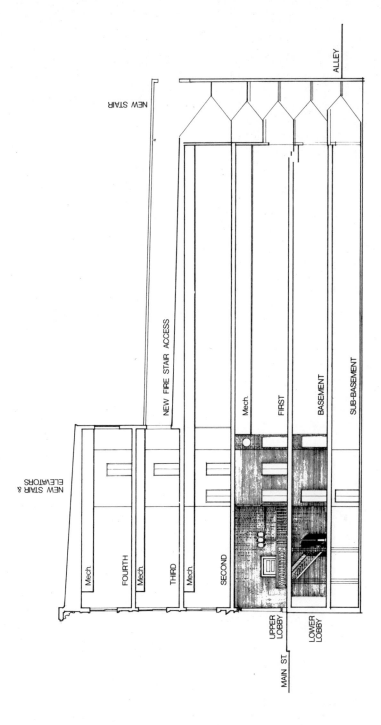

FIGURE 19-2 Elevation.

193

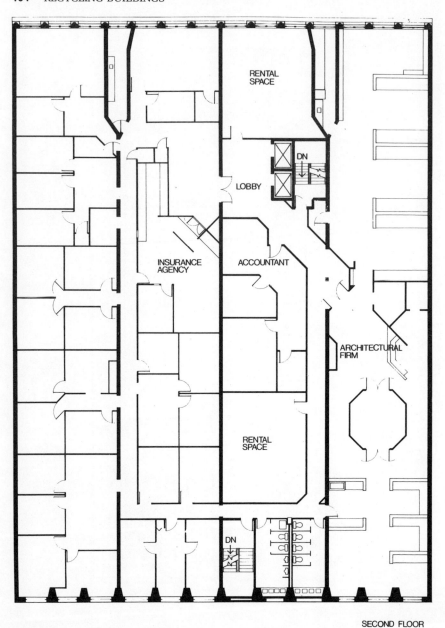

SECOND FLOOR

0   5   10   15

FIGURE 19-3   Second-floor plan.

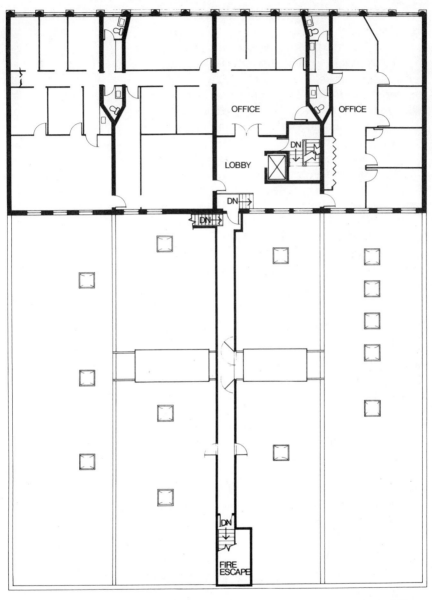

THIRD FLOOR

0   5   10   15

FIGURE 19-4   Third-floor plan.

architect is to retain the best of the old while at the same time modernizing the structure to meet present standards for light, heat, ventilation, air conditioning, plumbing, interior finishes, etc.

It was decided that the exterior would be completely refurbished and retained as is. There are very few ironfronts left, and these buildings are a historic monument. The broken cast iron was replaced by recasting new pieces. This was done by Stephen Baird, AIA, of Salt Lake City, an acknowledged expert in this field. As the four separate buildings were to be used as one, a single front entrance had to be designed with minimum disturbance to the architecture.

The entire electrical, plumbing, and heating systems had to be designed to code. Proper ventilation and air conditioning was an essential. New elevators and exitways were designed. The structure and the floors and walls had to be strengthened, and new finishes were required to meet modern requirements.

All the architecture and engineering was reduced to line drawings and outline specifications so that a builder could estimate the cost of the construction.

The Builder and the Budget Cost Study

After the architects had prepared line drawings and outline specifications and had a physical survey of the buildings made, the next step was to obtain an accurate estimate of what the cost of the recycling would be. To accomplish this the architects, who were now partners in the venture, employed a man who had been construction manager for a large construction company and who was thoroughly familiar with construction costs. This cost study is a model of what such a study should be. Every trade is broken down into its components, and each component is priced separately. An example of the carpentry trade category is given in Table 19-4.

The estimate, which included temporary protection, utilities, field supervision, etc., and the cost for complying with OSHA regulations ($6000) totaled $1,160,000.

The Rental Broker

The architect chose the firm of Harrison and Bates, one of the foremost real estate brokers and building operators in Richmond, to make a rental survey. This firm has knowledge of the going rental rates and operating costs for downtown office buildings and was therefore able to advise what rentals would be obtainable and what operating costs and

TABLE 19-4 COST BREAKDOWN IN CARPENTRY CATEGORY

Item	Area, ft², or number	Unit cost	Total cost
Repair roof joists and deck	14,000	$0.50	$7,000
Repair floor joists and floors	54,968	0.25	13,742
Remove floor third and fourth floor level, lobby	1,250	0.50	625
New floor	900	2.00	1,800
Frame and deck, skylight openings	396	2.00	792
Stair openings	18	100.00	1,800
Elevator openings	10	75.00	750
Miscellaneous small openings	30	25.00	750
Cut out and reframe floors			1,200
Repair and realign wood posts in basement			800
Relevel floors in basement			1,280
Support for hung floor at second level	1,200	2.00	2,400
Wood blocking at new roof			800
Miscellaneous grounds and blocking			3,000
Millwork at front between cast-iron columns	12	50.00	600
Plywood underlayment for floors	54,968	0.45	24,735
Frame masonry openings for aluminum sash	37	12.00	444

taxes would be. Harrison and Bates also confirmed that there was an active market for office space and store rentals in a structure of this kind at this location.

The Decision

The owners of the original property and the architect, who was to be the leadman of the project, gathered all the available information and prepared a statement of cost, income, and expense. As shown in the pro forma statement (Table 19-6), the cash flow did not seem very impressive and showed a return of only 6.5 percent on the equity of $560,000, which was the book value of the property as is. The statement, however, was to be used for financing purposes and to an extent understated the rent roll and overstated the expense. If this still showed a return on equity after all expense and debt-service costs were deducted, it should be impressive to a financial institution—and it was. Besides the 6.5 percent return was a vast improvement on the return earned before the recycling. It was therefore decided to proceed with the financing of the construction loan and the permanent mortgage and the architect-engineer proceeded to develop the working drawings and full specifications.

FIGURE 19-5 Refurbished exterior as it now looks.

19-7 THE FINANCING

Inquiries were started by a mortgage broker among various banks, insurance companies, REITs, and private lenders. The most receptive lender was the First and Merchants National Bank, whose headquarters is immediately adjacent to the project. The terms of the construction loan, which was closed in July 1975, was for $1.4 million at 3½ percent over the prime rate, this rate to continue until a permanent loan was closed, at which time the interest would be reduced to 2¾ percent over prime. Payouts were to be made monthly on the architect's certification less a 10 percent holdback.

With this construction loan in hand, the owners approached several insurance companies whose business is long-term mortgages. The Aetna Life took a 25-year mortgage in the sum of $1.4 million at an interest rate of 9⅝ percent plus 2 percent at the start. These are high interest rates, but the recycling of buildings has not yet been accepted as a normal mortgage risk compared with existing or well-located new construction. As more and more recycling projects become financially successful, it can be foreseen that interest rates will be comparable to those for new construction.

The pro forma statement which was filed with the applications for the construction and permanent loans is shown in Fig. 19-6 and Tables 19-5 and 19-6.

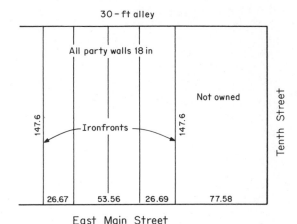

FIGURE 19-6 Plot plan accompanying pro forma application for mortgage.

19-8 THE ARCHITECT'S CONTRACT

The owners of the four ironfront buildings involved in this project chose the architectural firm of Glave, Newman and Anderson to make the initial studies of the property. The owners' instructions were to find the most architecturally attractive and the most economic way of recycling the property to make it appealing to prospective office and store renters. The buildings would have to be completely modernized so that top rents could be obtained while at the same time retaining their individualized appeal.

The first contract was made on the basis of professional fee plus expenses (AIA Form B331). An initial payment of $10,000 was made, and expenses were to be paid for as incurred. Labor was to be paid for at time plus one and a half. The architects had a structural and mechanical survey made and then produced line drawings and outline specifi-

TABLE 19-5 COST ESTIMATE

Amount requested, $1,400,000, 25 years	
Land area, 15,811 ft², purchase price, $560,000	
Rentable area of completed project, 60,416 ft²	
Cost of land	$560,000
Construction cost	$1,250,000
Architect and engineer	118,000
Taxes and insurance during construction	24,000
Miscellaneous utilities, advertising, accounting	14,000
Interest during construction and other expenses	90,000
Total cost	$2,056,000

TABLE 19-6 IRONFRONTS PRO FORMA, JULY 11, 1975

Cost:
  Land cost (14,600 ft² at $19.52/ft²) $ 285,000
  Cost of existing building:
    69,600 ft² at $3.75/ft²   275,000
    59,500 ft² at $19.32/ft²   1,160,000
  Payable to S. Douglas Fleet for land
    acquisition   70,000
  Other expenses (see Schedule A)   192,130
    Estimated total cost $1,982,130
Depreciation value $1,567,095
Financing:
  Interest rate, 9¾ at 27 years; constant
    10.6
  Permanent loan, cost of construction
    plus expenses $1,400,000
  Equity investment   560,000
  Net income before debt service $ 334,516
    Debt service $148,400
    Operating cost (Schedule B)   149,615
         298,015
    Net income   36,501
    Based on $560,000 equity,
    6.5% return

Schedule A

Architectural fees	$ 25,000
Legal	15,000
Mortgage fee	15,000
Miscellaneous	15,000
Interest on construction loan:	
First year, 3½ above prime, 10½ ×	
$1,4000,000 × 50%	73,500
Second year, $1,400,000 × 3 months	
× 10%	35,000
Taxes:	
$4250 × 1.88	7,990
$1500 × 1.98 × 2 months	5,640
Net	$192,130

Schedule B: annual expense projections

Management, 6% × $334,516 × 80% −	
3% of $39,500	$ 18,885
Insurance and taxes, 59,500 ft² × $0.65	38,350
Janitorial, 25,000 ft² × $0.55	19,800
Janitorial supplies, 36,000 ft² × $0.04	1,440
Lamps, 59,500 ft² × $0.01	595
Elevator (full service)	3,600

TABLE 19-6   IRONFRONTS PRO FORMA, JULY 11, 1975 (*Continued*)

HVAC, 59,500 ft^2 × $0.07	4,165
Plumbing, 59,500 ft^2 × $0.01	595
Electrical, 59,500 ft^2 × $0.02	1,180
Extermination	300
Refuse, 47,000 ft^2 × $0.02	940
Electricity, water, and sewer, 46,800 ft^2 × $1.25	58,750
Miscellaneous, 59,500 ft^2 × $0.02	1,180
Total	$149,615

	Schedule B: income projections		
Floor	Area, ft^2	Rental rate	Total rental
Subbasement	12,700	$ 2.25	$ 28,100
Basement	12,670	5.25	69,575
Ground	1,850	8.75	16,187
	6,847	10.00	68,470
	3,803	6.75	25,670
Second	12,731	6.75	85,935
Third	4,260	6.75	28,755
Fourth	4,360	6.75	29,430
			$352,122

$352,122 × 95% occupancy rate = $334,516 = gross income

cations. Some preliminary bids were obtained, but the project seemed to be coming to a standstill. It was at this point that the architects entered the partnership and invested their fee for completing the working drawings and specifications as payment for a partnership in Ironfront Associates. The architects have also moved their office to this location and serve as managers of the project.

19-9   THE FINAL PLANS AND SPECIFICATIONS

General Requirements

This division of the specifications refers to the overall performance of the work. There are sections on temporary facilities, substitutions of material, changes in the work, extra work, and project cleanup.

Demolition

The demolition specification calls for the following work:

Remove all interior partitions, wall and floor finishes, and ceilings unless otherwise indicated

Remove existing street-level storefronts, as shown on drawings, and carefully preserve the remaining fronts

Dismantle and remove existing telephone, gas, plumbing, mechanical, and electrical systems; coordinate with proper authorities to terminate piping and wiring as required

Maintain those utilities required for construction

Remove existing wood windows as indicated on drawings

Dismantle and remove existing elevators, dumbwaiters, stairs, and exterior fire escapes

Shore and reinforce all areas left in weakened condition

Store salvageable materials in a protected area

Cast-in-Place Concrete

All concrete to be 3000 lb/in² after 28 days. Concrete for footings for new steel columns to support new lobby floor. Pour 4-in reinforced subbasement floor slab in two buildings to match existing slab in other two buildings. Pour 2½-in reinforced lobby-floor slab. Concrete new elevator pits and all stairway landing slabs. Concrete treads of new steel-pan stairs.

Masonry

Brick of matching color to be used to patch all existing brick party walls and other exposed brick faces. Walls of elevator shafts to be of concrete block with exposed brick facing. Street-floor lobby to be paved with brick on poured-concrete slab. Windows in exterior rear wall to be bricked up with matching brick where shown on plan. Rear wall of fourth floor of one building to be repaired and rear fourth floor wall of three other buildings to be completely rebuilt with new brick and concrete-block wall.

Structural Steel, Steel Joists, and Miscellaneous Metal

Structural-steel columns and beams are used to support the street-floor lobby and to frame an ornamental stair to the basement. Structural-steel beams are used to reinforce or to replace the wood center beams which support the existing floor joists. All openings cut through the brick party walls are supported by two 6-in H lintels (note that only half the wall is to be removed at one time). Steel stairs to have pan-type treads and to be designed for 150 lb/ft² load.

Steel joists are open-web H series. They are used on the first floor, in conjunction with the structural steel, to support the entrance-lobby floor and on the roof to support the wood rafters.

Structural steel is used to frame openings in the roof of the third floor for new air-conditioning equipment and to furnish support for the equipment.

Rough Carpentry

All the structural wood floor joists are to be inspected and reinforced or replaced where necessary. The roof structure is to be reinforced with new wood joists and resheathed where necessary. New wood blocking is necessary for the support of the new mechanical units on the third-floor roof. All exposed wood is to be pressure-treated with wood preservative.

Building Insulation

Exterior walls are to be insulated with 2-in glass-fiber batts with vapor barrier, which is to be covered with ⅝-in dry wall over furring strips.

Roof insulation to be perlite-type 1½-in-thick surface-coated board with a C factor of 0.24. There is also existing insulation in the air space between the existing ceiling of the top floor and the roof.

Roofing and Flashing

Roofing is specified as three-ply asphalt and coated asbestos felt with a 10-year renewable guarantee. Through-wall flashing is of copper-bonded asphalt-saturated cloth. Cap flashing is of stainless steel. Through-wall flashing is specified for all exterior door and window heads. There are two sets of gutters and downspouts at the rear. One is for the fourth floor front position and one set is for the two-story roof at the rear. All gutters and downspouts are specified as galvanized.

Doors, Frames, and Storefronts

All doors and frames, except as noted, are specified as hollow metal except the doors at the storefronts on Main Street, which are of solid-core wood. Storefronts are of aluminum, and the specification is based on Kawneer. Doors to stairs and fire passages and exit doors are to be Underwriter's-labeled. All interior wood doors to be 1¾-in solid core with hollow metal frames.

Windows, Frames, and Glazing

The windows in the rear exterior wall of the four-story front section are specified as extruded-aluminum single-hung and factory-glazed. Air infiltration is specified not to exceed 0.079 ft^3/(min)(ft) at 1.56 lb/ft^2. All existing wood windows are specified to be repaired where necessary. Glazing is specified to be tempered Herculite or Ruf-Flex for openings as shown and double-thick standard glass in the windows.

Furring and Partitions

All furred walls are to be covered with ½-in wallboard. All fire corridors are specified to be of ⅝-in fire-rated gypsum wallboard on two sides of steel studs. All other partitions of ½-in gypsum wallboard on steel studs.

Acoustical Ceilings

All ceilings are specified to be hung exposed grid with noncombustible 2-hr-rated acoustic lay-in mineral fiber. Ceiling to be of 24 by 48 by ⅝-in boards with travertine finish.

Ceramic Tile and Resilient Flooring

All toilet rooms are specified to be 4¼- by 4¼-in matte-glazed tile for walls and floor tile as selected laid in portland-cement grout.

All floors are specified to be of 12- by 12-in vinyl asbestos tile ⅛ in.

Exterior Finish

The cast-iron front was repaired, and then a sandblasting operation was specified followed by two coats of lead and oil paint. Exterior wooden sash were to be painted with two coats.

Plumbing

The plumbing system is entirely new. Hot and cold water are galvanized wrought iron, and wastes and vents are cast iron. There are men's and women's toilets on every floor, including the subbasement. The fixture count is in compliance with code. Hot water is supplied by one 30-gal and one 40-gal electric hot-water heater in basement.

Heating, Ventilating, and Air Conditioning

There were two small existing air-conditioning compressors in the basement floor together with some ductwork which were salvaged. There are four additional air-conditioning units, of which two are located on the second-floor roof and two on the fourth-floor roof. These units consist of electrically driven centrifugal-type compressors. The refrigerant is cooled by an evaporative condenser mounted on an extension roof. The heating and cooling are also helped by a heat pump.

Air on the first three floors is distributed by ducts to linear ceiling diffusers, each of which has an electric reheat coil and all of which are controlled by thermostats. Heating is accomplished by the use of electric unit heaters mounted above the hung ceiling. The space above the hung ceiling is used as a return plenum. Square diffusers are used in the ceiling of the fourth floor.

The entire duct system is firesafed in accordance with code.

Electrical

Service is brought into the building through a transformer vault located in the subbasement at the rear. The service is 277/480 V, three-phase, four-wire.

There is an electrical equipment room in the rear of the basement floor.

Lighting fixtures are 24 by 48 in, four-tube set in the hung ceiling.

19-10   THE CONSTRUCTION CONTRACT

It was decided to employ a general contractor as a construction manager. For this purpose the construction firm headed by the man who had made the budget cost study was chosen. The A. McA. Heyward Co. was employed on a contract cost of work plus fee (AIA Form 111) to manage the construction for a fee not to exceed $100,000 plus a 30 percent share of any savings under the budget figure.

The architects themselves, with the advice of the construction manager, let all the subcontracts. The plumbing, heating, ventilating, air-conditioning, and electrical contract were let to a single contractor, who as a condition of his contract performed the design work for these trades.

The application and certificate for payment (Fig. 19-7), dated May 31, 1977, shows that the original contract sum of $1,160,000 was increased by tenant change work and change orders to $1,472,777.99. Some of the tenant change work was paid for by the tenants.

19-11 MARKETING THE PROJECT

Because of the attendant publicity about the ironfronts, the project was well known to start with. The owners employed Harrison & Bates as rental brokers and managing agents. An attractive brochure used as a

---

APPLICATION AND CERTIFICATE FOR PAYMENT   *AIA DOCUMENT G702*

PROJECT: (name, address) THE IRONFRONT BUILDING / 1007-13 East Main Street / Richmond, Virginia

ARCHITECT: GLAVE, NEWMAN, ANDERSON AND ASSOCIATES, INC.

ARCHITECT'S PROJECT NO: 23-72

TO (Owner) IRONFRONT ASSOCIATES / THE IRONFRONTS / 1011 East Main Street / Richmond, Virginia

CONTRACTOR: HEYWARD CONSTRUCTION CO., INC.

CONTRACT FOR:

APPLICATION DATE: June 13, 1977   APPLICATION NO: 20

ATTN: Mr. James M. Glave

PERIOD FROM: 4-25-77   TO 5-31-77

CHANGE ORDER SUMMARY

Application is made for Payment, as shown below, in connection with the Contract. Continuation Sheet, AIA Document G702A, is attached.

The present status of the account for this Contract is as follows:

Change Orders approved in previous months by Owner –	ADDITIONS $	DEDUCTIONS $
TOTAL	86,409,17	

Subsequent Change Orders	
Number	Approved (date)

TOTALS	
Net change by Change Orders	$ 86,409,17

State of: Virginia   ~~County of~~ City of Richmond

The undersigned Contractor certifies that the Work covered by this Application for Payment has been completed in accordance with the Contract Documents, that all amounts have been paid by him for Work for which previous Certificates for Payment were issued and payments received from the Owner, and that the current payment shown herein is now due.

Contractor:

By: _Earl Odum_ Date: 6/13/77

ORIGINAL CONTRACT SUM. . . . . $ 1,160,000.00
    Net Change by Tenant Changes 167,937.42
    Net change by Change Orders . . . . $ 86,409.17
    Net Change by Approved Extras 8,431.40

CONTRACT SUM TO DATE. . . . . $ 1,472,777.99

TOTAL COMPLETED & STORED TO DATE . . . . $ 1,307,500.75
  (Column G on G702A)

RETAINAGE_____ % . . . . $ –0–
or as noted in Column I on G702A

TOTAL EARNED LESS RETAINAGE . . . . $ 1,307,500.75

LESS PREVIOUS CERTIFICATES FOR PAYMENT. . . $ 1,292,759.59

CURRENT PAYMENT DUE. . . . . $ 14,741.16

Subscribed and sworn to before me this _____ day of _____ 19___

Notary Public:

My Commission expires:

In accordance with the Contract and this Application for Payment the Contractor is entitled to payment in the amount shown above

☐ OWNER
☐ ARCHITECT
☐ CONTRACTOR

Architect:

By: ☐

This Certificate is not negotiable. It is payable only to the payee named herein and its issuance, payment and acceptance are without prejudice to any rights of the Owner or Contractor under their Contract.

AIA DOCUMENT G702 ● APPLICATION AND CERTIFICATE FOR PAYMENT ● MARCH 1971 EDITION ● AIA®
©1971 ● THE AMERICAN INSTITUTE OF ARCHITECTS 1735 NEW YORK AVE., N. W.,WASHINGTON, D. C. 20006

FIGURE 19-7 Application certificate for payment.

FIGURE 19-8   Interior view

mailing piece was followed by newspaper advertisements and intensive canvassing of the kind of office used that would be attracted to the individuality of this kind of project (Fig. 19-8). Although the project is not yet fully completed, it is 62 percent rented with every prospect for full occupancy.

19-12   MANAGEMENT

The managing agents set up a maintenance schedule which is largely expressed in Exhibit B of Table 19-6. They collect the rents, pay all the bills, and collect their brokerage and management fee monthly. A statement of income and expense is rendered as of the fifteenth of every month. The balance of income over expense is set aside as a reserve to pay taxes and the debt service.

19-13 FORECAST OF PROSPECTIVE INCOME

Table 19-7 shows a projected income at 95 percent occupancy of 10.9 percent on the equity. This is before depreciation, so that certainly for the first several years of operation the income will be tax-free. This is typical of every recycling that has been well thought out with due regard for the principals of successful investment in real estate.

Recycling saves resources and can be quite profitable.

The pro forma statement submitted to Aetna as part of the request for the mortgage (Table 19-6) shows a net income of $36,501, or 6.5 percent on the equity of $560,000 (the cost of the land and original buildings.) This is not a very attractive return for any would-be investor. Although the project is not yet fully completed and is only 62 percent rented, the monthly management statements prepared by Harrison and Bates begin to show a trend which can be expressed in the forecast shown in Table 19-7.

TABLE 19-7   FORECAST OF INCOME, EXPENSE, AND RETURN ON INVESTMENT

Income:		
Rents are $0.25 to $0.50/ft^2 higher than forecast of $325,000; add $0.35/ft^2 for 59,000 ft^2 = $20,000, for a rent roll of $372,000:		
$372,000 × 0.95 (5% for vacancy)		$353,400
Expense:		
Maintenance and operating expense on pro forma, including insurance and taxes $149,615, or $2.52/ft^2, which can be reduced by at least $0.10/ft^2 when building is in full operation		
	$149,615	
59,000 × $0.10	5,900	
	$144,000	
Debt service	148,000	
		292,000
Net income (represents 10.9% on the equity)		$ 61,000

20

CASE STUDY FOUR:

WEYERBACHER TERRACE

INDIANAPOLIS, INDIANA

This is a study of the recycling of a hospital (St. Vincent's) for use as a low-rent housing project under Section 8 of the HUD-FHA regulations with mortgage insurance and rent subsidies provided by these federal agencies.

20-1 HOW THE PROJECT ORIGINATED

This project started because the developer's attention was called to it. Some time in 1970 the administrators of St. Vincent's Hospital, built in 1911, felt that it had outgrown its facilities and that its present location was no longer suited for a hospital. In addition, because of the age and layout of the buildings, the cost of operation and maintenance had become too high. In February 1972 a realtor called the developer to say that the hospital plant was for sale. Federal Property Management Corporation, based in Dayton, Ohio, has an excellent record as a developer in recycling buildings. Federal was interested and started negotiations with the hospital.

20-2 THE TENTATIVE DECISION CONCERNING THE FINAL USE

From the very start all concerned realized that the hospital's location in a rather run-down residential area and the structural layout of the hospital buildings pointed toward its development as a low-rent residential project. As the negotiations for the sale continued, two decisions were made and carried out. The first was to employ an architect to perform preliminary layout work. Woollen Associates of Indianapolis had worked with the developer, and Lynn Molzan was designated to carry out the work, which was done on a speculative basis. The second decision was to start preliminary inquiries with HUD-FHA to determine whether FHA would insure a mortgage and whether under Section 8 and its subsidiary regulations the federal agency would grant rent subsidies to the project as a low-rent project for elderly low-income tenants. Because of the character of the area it was felt that only a low-rent subsidized project could succeed.

The agency will not consider an application until a great deal of legal and architectural work has been done and a comprehensive feasibility study has been made. If the project is not approved, this work may have been done without adequate compensation. Nevertheless, Federal pursued the project and finally obtained an approval. In January 1973 the hospital moved to its new location.

20-3 CITY DATA

Although in this case the economic and other background information regarding Indianapolis is not particularly pertinent, the following digest would be important in every other kind of commercial or residential recycling and is given here as a model of the information an entrepreneur should have before making a final decision.

Geographical Location[1]

Indianapolis is the capital of Indiana as well as the county seat of Marion County. It is the geographical, economic, political, and cultural

---

[1]The following information on geographical location, population, transportation, industry and business, retail sales, employment, education, health facilities, and trend is based on data collected by the Mortgage Department of the Equitable Life Assurance Society of the United States and used with their permission.

TABLE 20-1 POPULATION OF INDIANAPOLIS AND MARION COUNTY

Year	Indianapolis	Change, %	Marion County	Change, %
1950	427,173		551,777	
1960	467,258	+12	690,162	+25
1970	744,624	+59*	793,590	+15
1975†	778,400	+5	828,000	+4

*Reflects effects of Unigov.
†Estimated.

center of the state of Indiana. The city is located 181 mi from Chicago, 106 mi from Cincinnati, 171 mi from Columbus, 111 mi from Louisville, 278 mi from Detroit, and 235 mi from St. Louis.

Population

Indianapolis has had a history of steady expansion. Its central location and planned design, without any geographical boundaries, has enabled it to grow in all directions in a well-balanced pattern. On January 1, 1970 through Unigov, the city annexed all suburbs (except Beech Grove, Lawrence, and Speedway), thereby making it the eleventh largest city in the United States. Latest U.S. Census population figures are given in Table 20-1.

The Indianapolis standard metropolitan statistical area comprises eight counties. The estimated future population for the Indianapolis SMSA is shown in Table 20-2.

TABLE 20-2 POPULATION OF INDIANAPOLIS METROPOLITAN AREA

County	1960 census	1970 census	1975	1980	1985	1990
Marion	690,162	793,590	840,000	895,500	955,300	1,040,000
Boone	27,543	30,870	32,100	34,000	35,800	37,700
Hamilton	40,132	54,532	63,200	75,500	87,500	99,800
Hancock	26,665	35,096	39,800	45,300	51,900	59,000
Hendricks	40,896	53,974	59,000	64,600	71,300	78,500
Johnson	43,704	61,138	68,700	76,000	90,600	97,000
Morgan	33,875	44,176	48,600	52,900	58,000	65,400
Shelby	34,093	37,797	38,600	40,100	42,800	44,700
Total SMSA	937,070	1,111,173	1,190,000	1,283,900	1,393,200	1,522,100

Transportation

Indianapolis, termed the "crossroads of America," is the confluence of Interstate Highways I-65, I-70, I-74 and I-465, six U.S. Highways, numbers 31, 36, 40, 52, 136, and 421, and six Indiana Highways, numbers 37, 37A, 67, 100, 135, and 431. These highways provide fast and easy access to all major cities in the Midwest.

Indianapolis International Airport, located on the west side of Indianapolis 1 mi west of the subject property, is served by six major airlines (TWA, Allegheny, American, Eastern, Delta, and Ozark) as well as two commuter lines and air-freight services. Formerly named Weir Cook Municipal Airport, it has recently been renamed to reflect its newly gained international status. A $25 million expansion and a continued land-acquisition plan will keep the airport in stride with the growing aviation needs of the Indianapolis area.

Conrail and Amtrak provide rail service to the Indianapolis area.

The city is a divisional terminal for two coast-to-coast motor-bus systems and seven interstate lines. Ten intrastate motor-coach lines connect with cities and towns throughout Indiana.

More than 100 motor-truck lines operate out of Indianapolis, 5 of them having their home offices in the city.

Industry and Business

Indianapolis is classified a class I industrial city. Marion County, with 653 plants and a total of $6.288 billion in annual total shipments, ranks twenty-seventh in manufacturing activities in the nation. The city's industry and services are widely diversified, with approximately 1100 manufacturing firms producing more than 1200 different commodities. The products manufactured include pharmaceutical and biological products, telephone apparatus, truck and airplane engines, road-building equipment, automobile plants, and food products. Government facilities include the U.S. Army Finance Center and School at Fort Benjamin Harrison and the Naval Avionics Facility, two of Indianapolis' major employers. Other major employers are listed in Table 20-3.

Business is represented by more than 7000 retail firms. More than 70 insurance companies maintain home offices in Indianapolis. Six Indianapolis banks with resources exceeding $6 billion operate 196 offices throughout the county in addition to 10 savings and loans operating 45 offices. Office and hotel space was expanded by the completion in 1977 of the $50 million Merchant's Plaza, a mixture of hotel (Hyatt-Regency), office, and commercial. There are five major retail stores in downtown Indianapolis, and retailers keep pace with

TABLE 20-3 MAJOR EMPLOYERS

Company	No. of employees
Eli Lilly & Company	27,400
Detroit Diesel Allison Division (GMC)	13,000
Western Electric Company, Inc.	7,570
Chevrolet Motor Division	5,300
RCA Consumer Electronics	4,800
Ford Motor Company	3,990
Chrysler Corp., electrical plant	3,550
International Harvester	3,400

suburban growth through shopping centers. There are two regional shopping centers on the north side of the city and one each on the south, east, and west sides, as well as numerous community and neighborhood centers.

Retail Sales

The median effective buying income of the 3,899,000 households in the Indianapolis SMSA is $14,304. Increases in retail sales are shown in Table 20-4.

Employment

According to Indiana Employment Securities Division reports, employment of Indianapolis area residents in 1977 was at an all-time high and moderate increases in employment are expected during the coming months. At the same time, unemployment decreased. Compared with 1 year ago, manufacturing employment was 2600 higher in mid-May, and nonmanufacturing employment showed increases also.

Table 20-5 is a comparison of the average unemployment for Indianapolis, Indiana, and the United States for the years indicated. The Indianapolis metropolitan area has historically enjoyed a favorable labor climate with comparatively few strikes and labor unrest. This feature has been attractive to industry.

TABLE 20-4 RETAIL SALES IN INDIANAPOLIS (000 OMITTED)

Item	1972	1975	Increase, %
Total retail sales, Indianapolis SMSA	$2,720,531	$3,675,179	+35
Food	510,166	692,432	+36
Eating and drinking places	223,311	332,656	+49

TABLE 20-5   COMPARISON OF UNEMPLOYMENT IN INDIANAPOLIS, THE
STATE, AND THE NATION

	1973	1974	1975	1976	4/77	5/77
Indianapolis SMSA	4.2	4.8	6.4	6.7	5.7	6.0
Indiana	4.3	5.2	8.6	6.1	5.0	5.0
United States	4.9	5.6	8.5	7.7	7.0	6.9

Education

Indianapolis has an excellent public and private school system, offering programs from kindergarten through adult education. Three uni-
versities and one college are located in Indianapolis; Indiana Univer-
sity-Purdue University at Indianapolis (IUPUI) has an enrollment of
18,000 and offers more than 100 degree programs. Butler University, a
private school offering degrees in liberal arts and sciences, has an
enrollment of 4300 full- and part-time students; Indiana Central University has an enrollment of 3600 and Marion College a student population of 1000. Special instruction is available at the Noble School for
Retarded Children and the Indiana State School for the Blind and
Indiana State School for the Deaf. Indiana Vocational Technical College is a constantly expanding trade school. Indiana University's medical and dental schools are located at Indianapolis as well as a branch of
its School of Law.

Health Facilities

Indianapolis has a wide range of health-related organizations and
resources geared to local and statewide services. There are 17 licensed
hospitals, 12 of which are general hospitals and 3 are for the treatment
of psychiatric patients. Indiana University Medical Center, which
includes 5 hospitals and 80 clinics, provides the most complete and
comprehensive care in all fields of medicine and several of the dental
specialties. One of the most prestigious teaching centers in the country,
it is the largest patient-care complex in the state.

Trend

In view of all the foregoing, including the diversification in industry,
business, and government as well as the facilities for future growth and
development, it appears reasonable that the present trend of growth
and expansion will continue. The long-term outlook for Indianapolis is
upward.

20-4   THE SITE

The property is located on the square block bounded by Illinois Street, 26th Street, Capitol Ave., and Fall Creek Boulevard (Fig. 20-1). It is 2½ mi from the business center of the city, which is approximately at Illinois and Washington Streets. The property consists of four buildings, the main hospital building, the nurses' quarters, the former convent, and the power house. There are parking areas on both sides of the main building, which faces on Fall Creek Boulevard, and there is a large parking area across Capitol Avenue.

The land area of the main site, which measures approximately 573 by 350 ft, is over 200,000 ft².

The approximate gross area of the buildings to be recycled is over 300,000 ft².

20-5   SURVEY OF THE BUILDINGS

The architects employed a structural engineer to survey the buildings for structural integrity. They themselves surveyed the buildings for usable layouts, fire safety, mechanical and electrical installations, exit facilities, elevators, stairways, architectural finishes, moistureproofing, etc.

The buildings (Figs. 20-2 to 20-4) were found to be structurally sound. The poured-concrete foundation showed no signs of settlement. The brick and terra cotta exterior walls were in excellent condition. The floor arches are of long-span reinforced terra cotta and concrete

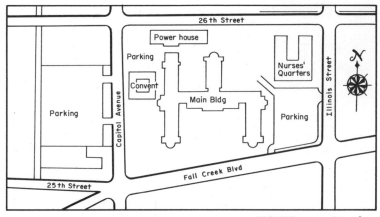

FIGURE 20-1   Site plan.

FIGURE 20-2 Front of main building from Fall Creek Parkway.

FIGURE 20-3 Power house; with chimney, boilers, etc., removed and window removed, it is now two floors of apartments.

FIGURE 20-4   Former nurses' quarters. The former chapel (arched windows) has been divided. One half is now a two-story community room, and the other half has been divided by a new floor to make two floors of apartments.

(more fireproof than present-day construction). The corridors were floored with terrazzo. The existing stairways and exit facilities were of the proper construction and of sufficient size to meet the present code (Fig. 20-5). Only four new stairways had to be added to meet the new requirements for the location of exit facilities. There were sufficient elevators. The buildings had been constructed in 1911 as a hospital and had met the then existing building code. They were of excellent construction and had been well maintained. The FHA required as a condition of its approval that the HVAC and plumbing systems be almost completely renewed and that a completely new electrical system be installed. FHA also required that all windows be aluminum, double-glazed and double-hung (Fig. 20-6).

The construction necessary to create an apartment complex would consist of gutting the interiors by removing all interior partitions; creating residential units by erecting new partitions; and installing new HVAC, plumbing, and electrical systems to meet the needs of residential users, including kitchens, bathrooms, electrical convenience outlets, stair and general lighting, etc. Floor plans before and after renovation are shown in Fig. 20-7.

FIGURE 20-5   Grand stairway, retained from original construction. (*By permission from House and Home magazine, November 1976, copyright by McGraw-Hill, Inc.*)

20-6   ZONING AND BUILDING CODES

Zoning

The project is located in a residential area, which allows anything from single-family dwellings on 30-ft lots to multiple dwelling units. There is also a scattering of commercial zoning on the main thoroughfares. These zones allow light manufacturing, gas stations, repair shops, etc.

The zoning of the site was originally changed from a hospital zone to a D8 residential. It was found, however, that if the existing hospital building was to be developed into the maximum number of low-rent dwelling units, the D8 zone was too restrictive. An appeal was made to change the zone to D9, and because there are numerous D9 zones in the immediate vicinity and because this project fitted into the city's need for low-rent housing, the appeal was granted. This allowed the devel-

FIGURE 20-6   Aluminum-framed thermal windows conserve energy and reduce internal condensation. (*By permission from House and Home magazine, November 1976, copyright by McGraw-Hill, Inc.*)

oper to take the maximum advantage of the buildings and the site. A zoning map is shown in Fig. 20-8.

The regulations for the D9 zone are titled "development standards". Building heights are unlimited. Depending on the height of the buildings, the floor-area ratio runs from 0.50 to 2.70. The open-space ratios and other ratios such as maximum and minimum livability space also vary. Parking space, however, remains one space for each dwelling unit.

Building Code

Indianapolis Building Code is an adaptation of the Uniform Code,[1] which varies only slightly from the BOCA code. The city also follows the NFPA Code 101.

[1]Published by the International Conference of Building Officials, 5360 S. Workman Mill Road, Whittier CA 90601.

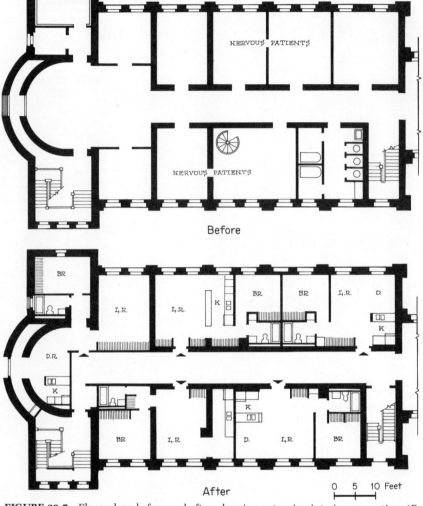

FIGURE 20-7 Floor plans before and after, showing extensive interior renovation. (*By permission from House and Home magazine, November 1976, copyright by McGraw-Hill, Inc.*)

20-7 THE MARKETING SURVEY

One of the requirements of HUD-FHA is a marketing or feasibility survey. The actual surveys made are shown in Tables 20-6 and 20-7. This survey shows a vacancy of only 5.32 percent in all the limited-income units surveyed. It definitely shows that there is a market for such units.

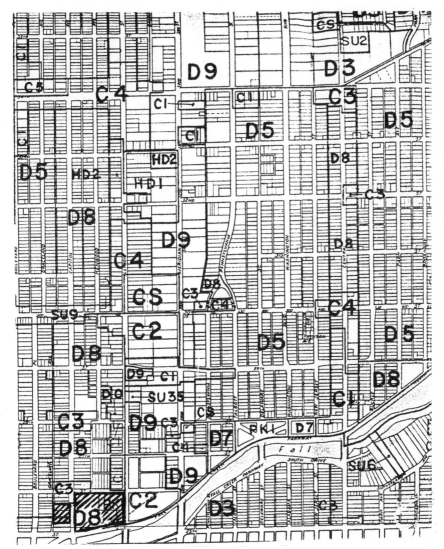

FIGURE 20-8   Portion of zoning map showing the site area (marked D8 at the lower left-hand corner).

The sample surveys shown in Table 20-7 are of completed Section 236 (now Section 8) rent-supplement, low-income housing. Several other projects were surveyed, but these two were sufficient to show that this project would command a ready market for the type of housing it was prepared to provide.

TABLE 20-6   LIMITED-INCOME UNITS*

District	Zip-code numbers	Total number	Vacant Units	%
Northwest	46260, 68, 78, 90	612	44	7.19
Northeast	46205, 20, 40, 50, 56, 80	300	0	0
East	46218, 19, 26, 29, 36	2707	185	6.83
Southeast	46203, 27, 39, 59	498	20	4.02
West	46208, 22, 24, 34, 54	996	0	0
Downtown	46201, 02, 04, 21, 25	586	73	12.45
Greenwood	46142	358	0	0
		6057	322	5.32

*Prepared by Apartment Association of Indianapolis, Inc.

Neighborhood Survey

In addition to the marketing study, a neighborhood survey was made which contained the following headings:

Rehabilitated or recycled projects under Section 236 located within 1 mi radius of this project. There were no new projects.

The major employers in the community.

TABLE 20-7   SAMPLE SURVEYS OF SECTION 236 RENT-SUPPLEMENT LOW-INCOME HOUSING

Owner	Efficiency No.	Monthly rent*	One-bedroom No.	Monthly rent*	Two-bedroom No.	Monthly rent*	Total units
Academy Associates†	23	$79–$85	56	$106–$135	...	....	79
Savoy-Hoosier†	31	$88–$91	163	$103–$119	2	$137.50	196

Apartment	No. of applications on hand before completion	Date of permission to occupy	Date 95% occupancy reached	Approximate present occupancy, %	Applications pending
Academy	90	2/12/73	4/1/73‡	98	50
Hoosier	150	1/29/73	3/15/73‡	98	65
Savoy	110	4/4/73	7/1/73§	97	45

*40% rent supplement.

†All utilities paid.

‡45-day rent-up period.

†90-day rent-up period.

The number of households that would be eligible for this subsidized housing.

The number of welfare recipients and other low-income families (these figures can be obtained from social welfare agencies).

Social services available.

Schools (grade, high, parochial, others).

Medical facilities.

Transportation.

Churches.

Recreation (libraries, museums, cinemas, parks).

Shopping (food, clothing, drugstores, cleaners, etc.).

Minorities as a percentage of the area population.

Affirmative Fair-Housing Marketing Plans

As in all recycled projects under HUD-FHA insurance and subsidization, the sponsor must show that he has taken positive action to advertise the project to *both* minority and majority groups. The sponsor must fill out a HUD form to show his entire marketing effort. In this case there were double-column advertisements in the Sunday editions of the major newspapers. There were spot announcements on several radio stations, including several minority stations. There were announcements in churches, at citizen's forums on television, at senior-citizen centers, at human resources centers, at hospitals, and to the local housing authority.

A section in the HUD-FHA form relates to the employment and training of minority employees.

20-8 THE PLANS AND SPECIFICATIONS

General Conditions

This section calls for the use of the General Conditions as published by AIA Document A201 (April 1970 edition).

In addition and because this is an FHA-HUD low-rent housing project, the following sections are added:

In addition to the requirements set forth in "The AIA General Conditions," [the contractor shall comply with the following:] All work under this Contract shall comply with current codes, standards, and requirements of

Federal, State and local authorities for rehabilitation of residential properties in accordance with the intent of U.S. Department of Housing and Urban Development/FHA guidelines included in publication HUD PG-50. Copies may be obtained from Superintendent of Documents, U.S. Government Printing Office, Washington, D.C. 20402, or the local Federal Housing Administration Office.

AFFIRMATIVE ACTION PROGRAM

The General Contractor at the time of the scheduled "Preconstruction Conference" shall submit the following:

a. Furnish proof that minority contractors have been invited to bid.

b. If the contractors to be awarded contracts do not possess sufficient minority members in order to comply with affirmative action guidelines, show that these individuals and agencies have been contacted that might be in a position to refer and/or recommend minority workers.

Because this project was recycled under the auspices of HUD-FHA, the specifications had to equal or better FHA specifications for housing rehabilitation. These can be obtained at an HUD office (FHA Minimum Property Standards).

General Requirements

This section is the usual wrap-up of the contractor's duties, including safety, signs, scaffolding, material storage, workmanship, cleanup, temporary facilities, and temporary heat.

Demolition

The requirement for demolition is divided into several distinct parts.

One existing building is to be demolished to grade. All foundation walls are to be broken up to 1 ft 6 in below grade. Any floor slabs below grade and the basement slab are to be broken up in order to permit drainage. The remaining basement hole is to be filled with masonry debris only to 1 ft 6 in below grade. All other debris of any kind whatsoever is to be removed from the site.

In the buildings that are to remain all interior walls and all existing floor, wall, and ceiling finishes are to be removed, with the exception of those shown on the plans. Also all existing equipment including plumbing, electric, heating, piping, and fixtures are to be removed except as shown.

All windows are to be removed, but this must be coordinated with the installation of new windows.

Removal of existing roofing must be coordinated with the installation of new roofing and is the responsibility of the roofing contractor.

The contractor is allowed to keep all salvaged material except that specifically designated for reuse by the architect. This includes certain architectural artifacts.

All pollution-control regulations must be complied with.

Sitework

This section includes asphalt paving and curbs, landscaping, parking-lot work, and extermination. The latter calls for examination by qualified persons of all exterior surfaces for termites after demolition work is completed. It also calls for extermination services for rodent and insect control and the closing of all openings into the buildings by masonry or noncorrosive sheet metal. The owner provides a monthly extermination service after the initial one is completed by the contractor.

Concrete and Masonry

This portion of the specification refers to the concrete slabs, concrete reinforcement, and masonry partitions that must be erected for both structural reinforcement and for compliance with the fire code for multifamily dwellings. There are also several cases where a very high vertical space was divided into two floors.

It also calls for tuckpointing of all exterior masonry where required and specifically mentions the percentage of the masonry in each building that is to be so treated. Any amount over this must be approved by the architect and is to be paid for. (Note that this is an excellent way of limiting a bid by giving the contractor explicit instructions about the extent of the work.)

Miscellaneous Metals

This section covers the usual pipe railings, ladders, access doors, etc., of aluminum and steel. It also covers several steel-pan stairs added to cover present fire-code requirements for number and location of exits.

Steel Joists

All new floors are to be supported by open-web steel joists with crossed steel bridging. The joists that are supported by masonry are to be placed on steel bearing plates anchored to the masonry. The joists bearing on steel are to be welded to the steel supports.

Carpentry and Millwork

Carpentry is divided into two parts. The rough carpentry includes blocking, nailers, framing, furring, grounds, etc., as well as all temporary protection. The finished carpentry and millwork includes furnishing and installing miscellaneous shelving, closet dividers, countertops (both wood and laminated plastic), finished wood or metal doorframes at the contractor's choice, and the installation of all finished hardware furnished by others.

All material that is specified is of excellent quality such as high-quality white pine or clear redwood for exterior trim, exterior-grade plywood for closures and soffits, paint/grade birch plywood for closet work, paint/grade birch for trim, etc.

Dampproofing

This section calls for trowel dampproofing of all grade walls which are adjacent to interior space and which are *exposed temporarily* during construction. It does not call for dampproofing existing below-grade walls, which are to be left undisturbed by the new construction.

Thermal Insulation

Thermal insulation is discussed in Sec. 20-9.

Roofing

Before writing this specification the architects employed roofing experts, who made a detailed survey of the existing conditions and then submitted a report with their recommendations for repairing and renewing the existing roofing to bring it back to a 20-year bondable condition. This report also went to the FHA.

The specification for the built-up roof calls for a 20-year bondable roof, using asbestos or organic felts and asphalt or coal-tar pitch. The sheet metal, depending on its location, may be galvanized steel, stainless steel, copper, or sheet lead. Concealed or built-in flashings (not exposed to weather) may also be of 3-oz copper-coated building paper.

Thermal insulation will be covered in Sec. 20-9.

Caulking and Sealants

This specification calls for caulking at window frames, louvers, vents, grilles, and vertical control joints; also horizontal joints in exterior concrete slabs, curbs, walks, and at door openings where interior and exterior slabs meet.

Hollow Metal Doors and Frames

Hollow metal doors and frames are specified where called for by the fire code. Underwriters-labeled doors are also called for at fire exits and at fire walls.

Wood Doors

Under the heading "carpentry" the subcontractors had the choice of using metal or wood frames in certain locations. Wood doors may be used in such locations. The plans contain a door schedule which designates what kind of door and frame is to be used where. Wood doors are specified to be flush hollow-core doors faced with finished Masonite or paint-grade birch.

Aluminum Windows

Windows are specified to be heavy-gauge, double-hung aluminum with a specified color finish and built in weatherstripping. The vent portion of all windows is screened.

There are a few single-hung and horizontal sliding windows; the specification calls for the vent section of such windows to be tilt-removable for cleaning.

The specification also describes how old windows are to be removed and replaced by the new.

Aluminum Entrances

The entrances to all the buildings are specified to have heavy extruded aluminum frames and extraduty aluminum doors. All anchors, bolts, and other fastenings are of corrosionproof metal. Doors are to be swung on offset pivots and to have special heavy-duty door closers. Glass is 1/4-in tempered plate set in neoprene gaskets. Aluminum finish is dark bronze Duranodic.

Entrance doors are also equipped with electric locks, further explained in Sec. 20-10.

FIGURE 20-9 Entrance to wing of hospital building showing new facade and protective awning. (*By permission from House and Home magazine, November 1976, copyright by McGraw-Hill, Inc.*)

Gypsum Drywall

All interior partitions are specified to be of gypsum wallboard with the following fire ratings:

Partition	Rating, h
Corridor walls	1
Party walls	1
Trash room and trash chute walls	2
Vertical shaft walls	2
Internal partitions	—

The thickness of the partitions and the wallboard is as follows:

Corridor walls and party walls. $3\frac{5}{8}$ in 25-gauge metal studs and runners; studs on 24-in centers; single-layer $\frac{5}{8}$-in fire-grade board and 1-in sound-attenuation blanket

Trash room. trash-chute walls and vertical shaft enclosures $3\frac{5}{8}$-in 25-gauge metal studs, on 24-in centers on metal runners; two layers $\frac{5}{8}$-in fire-grade board on outside and 1-in shaft-wall liner panels on inside

Internal partitions. 2½-in 25-gauge studs and runners; studs 24 in on center; single-layer ½-in board each side

Ceramic Tile

Ceramic tile 4¼ by 4¼ in cushion-edge type is specified for bathroom walls. The tile is specified to be installed on all sides of bathtubs to a height of 6 ft. It is to be installed in water-resistant organic-type adhesive over water-resistant wallboard.

Resilient Flooring and Base

The material is 12- by 12- by ³/₃₂-in vinyl asbestos floor tile specified to be installed in all living areas except the living rooms and dining rooms, which are carpeted.

Resilient base is of ⅛-in rubber or vinyl with premolded exterior corners. Stair treads are of resilient tile.

Acoustic Ceilings

Because of the more than normal clear height that existed in the hospital building the architect specified hung acoustic ceilings throughout. The ceilings consist of acoustic textured mineral boards ⅝ by 24 by 48 in wide, laid into an exposed T-bar system, T bars to be white-painted finish. Board is to be Underwriters-labeled for limited flame spread. Hung ceiling to extend into closets.

Painting and Finishing

The specified quality of the materials is above average. Dry-wall areas are specified to have two coats of latex alkyd flat and the surface in kitchens, baths, etc., to have two coats of interior latex semigloss enamel. Wood surfaces have one coat of enamel undercoater and one coat of latex alkyd semigloss enamel. All mechanical lines are specified to be color-coded. Exterior wood trim has one coat of exterior wood primer and one coat of exterior gloss enamel. Exterior concrete or stucco surfaces have two coats of waterproof paint in the color selected.

Miscellaneous Accessories

These specifications include a 24-in diameter 18-gauge steel trash chute and a garbage compactor; complete bathroom accessories including a surface-mounted 19 by 24-in medicine cabinet; mailboxes in building lobbies; prefabricated metal closet shelves; drapery tracks; and carpeting in living and dining areas.

Kitchen Equipment

There are sections on kitchen cabinets and countertops, electric ranges, refrigerators, and kitchen exhaust hoods.

The kitchen cabinets are finished with formica plastic laminate and are of excellent quality. The ranges are specified to have four surface burners and an oven and broiler and meet federal specifications. A 1-year warranty is called for. The refrigerators are specified to be of 11.5-ft³ minimum capacity and to be in accord with federal specifications for insulation, metal gauge, etc. A 1-year warranty is specified for the entire refrigerator and a 4-year warranty for the cooling unit. The kitchen exhaust hood is equipped with a fan and an activated-charcoal grease filter.

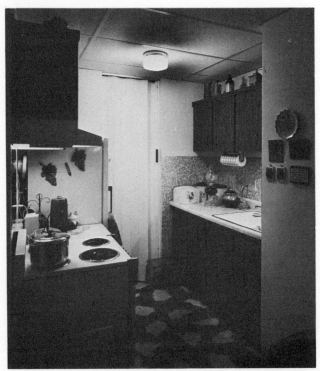

FIGURE 20-10 Typical kitchen. (*By permission from House and Home magazine, November 1976, copyright by McGraw-Hill, Inc.*)

Elevators

The specification calls for the removal of two existing elevators and one dumbwaiter and the rehabilitation of four others. The rehabilitation consists to a large extent of the replacement of worn parts and the installation of new cables, safeties, and collective-selective controls. The existing doorframes are reused, but new automatic doors are to be installed. The existing hoisting equipment is refurbished and reused.

Electrical

In accordance with the requirements of the FHA, all the electric wiring, risers, panels, main switchboards, etc., were replaced completely with new wiring and devices to meet the requirements of the National Electrical Code and the requirements of the local power company. Circuit wiring is 110/208 V, and wiring for HVAC units is 277/480 V.

Plumbing

FHA also required the replacement of all plumbing. The specifications called for standard-quality toilet fixtures (Fig. 20-11). Hot- and cold-water lines are copper. Hot water is circulated at 170°F from a hot-water heater. Wastes and vent lines are polyvinyl chloride and cast iron. All work is in accordance with the local code and with FHA specifications. There are laundry rooms in two of the buildings.

Heating, Ventilating, and Air Conditioning

The heating system (Fig. 20-12) was completely renewed with a new combination heating and air-conditioning system. Heating boilers circulate water at 95°F through a heater–air-conditioner unit located in each apartment. The heater-cooler units work on the heat-pump principle and use the hot water for heating in the winter and as a source of heat for air conditioning in the summer. A blower unit circulates the warm or cool air through ducts and diffusers into the various rooms in each apartment. Each unit is connected through flexible hoses with supply and return lines and to a condensate line. The cooling tower (evaporative condensers) is located in a courtyard.

It is the experience of the design engineers that properly adjusted and maintained heat-pump units are more economical to install than a conventional central system and more economical in their use of energy.

FIGURE 20-11 Typical bathroom.

20-9 ENERGY CONSERVATION

As the recycling planning proceeded, every effort was made by FHA-HUD, the architects, the engineers, and the owners to design and install proper insulation and energy-saving devices.

Insulation above top-floor apartment ceilings is 3½-in-thick blanket-type fiber glass.

Roof insulation is ¾-in-thick noncombustible compressed fiber glass.

Aluminum windows are double-glazed.

Aluminum frames and sash are equipped with a thermal break to eliminate the conduction of the exterior temperature to the interior.

FIGURE 20-12   Supplemental heating system comprising electric furnaces placed in each apartment. Resembling unit ventilators, the thermostatically controlled furnaces boost the temperature of hot water flowing through the heating coils. (*By permission from House and Home magazine, November 1976, copyright by McGraw-Hill, Inc.*)

Dry wall on existing exterior wall sections is applied over a 3½-in fiber-glass insulating blanket.

The heating and cooling by the heat-pump units is designed to be energy-saving.

20-10   SECURITY

The project is in a somewhat run-down neighborhood which has become stabilized—thanks in a large part to this project. However, it was thought best, especially in the case of a low-rent subsidized housing project, to build in and maintain maximum security.

A television camera is focused on every street-floor opening in every building. There are eleven closed-circuit television receivers under constant scrutiny in the main office (Fig. 20-13).

No one can enter a building without pressing certain coded numbers which are different for each apartment. The caller must then identify himself to the apartment occupant before the electric door release is activated. If no one is at home and the person does not have a key, he cannot get in. The office will not furnish entry to anyone.

Each apartment corridor door has an intrusion alarm which is activated by coded push buttons at each door. Unauthorized entry will set off an alarm.

20-11 PROJECT AMENITIES

Some apartments are duplex (Fig. 20-14). The project maintains a large meeting room (Fig. 20-15), several card or game rooms, laundry and dryer rooms (Fig. 20-16), and a convenience shop, which sells medical products, staple groceries, newspapers, magazines, tobacco, etc.

FIGURE 20-13 Rental office, showing television monitors providing surveillance of entrances and parking lots. (*By permission from House and Home magazine, November 1976, copyright by McGraw-Hill, Inc.*)

FIGURE 20-14 A duplex created from gym and auditorium in former nurses' quarters. (*By permission from House and Home magazine, November 1976, copyright by McGraw-Hill, Inc.*)

20-12 FINANCING

The construction financing was furnished by a lending institution with an FHA guarantee. The company was Advance Mortgage Co., of Minneapolis. The interim and permanent financing is by a limited partnership Urban Improvement Fund, Ltd. Most projects under HUD-FHA are financed in the same manner.

FHA insured a mortgage amounting to 90 percent of the certified cost consisting of land, original buildings, administrative costs, architectural costs, and construction.

The cost per square foot of the complete recycling was $12.20 compared with the $30 to $35 per square foot cost of type I construction in Indianapolis.

FIGURE 20-15 Community room formed from old chapel area.

FIGURE 20-16 Laundry room installed in hospital and nurses' buildings.

20-13   THE ARCHITECT'S AND BUILDER'S FEES

The architect's fee is set by FHA, which takes into consideration such items of cost as land improvement, building construction cost, general requirements, and general overhead. The amount of fee allowed compares favorably with fees charged by architects in conventional commercial work.

The builder's fee is based on a certain allowed amount of overhead plus the normal percentage amount that a builder would add to his estimate for builder's risk and profit. Like the architect's fee, the total amount allowed is in line with the usual builder's charges for conventional work.

The architects were Woollen Associates, of Indianapolis. The general contractor was Sheehan Construction Co., of Indianapolis.

20-14   RENTING THE PROJECT

Under the regulations set by HUD-FHA the sponsor of the project must make it known that such low-rent, subsidized housing is available. The sponsor must advertise the project for at least 60 days before its completion and must present FHA with a schedule of how and when these advertisements will appear. Depending on the groups to be reached, the advertisements may appear in foreign-language or minority newspapers or magazines and in foreign-language radio announcements that are known to appeal to minorities, the elderly, or other disadvantaged persons.

In this case, as in most Section 8 rehabilitations, the project was 100 percent rented before its completion. The number of applicants for the limited amount of such housing enables the sponsor to some small extent to avoid renting to the apparently disruptive and the destructive. Some sponsors in particularly poor neighborhoods have even requested advice from a committee composed of the minority toward which the project is oriented. It has been found that such committees tend to be more severely restrictive than any sponsor would dare to be.

The basic rentals start at $115 to $125 per month for efficiency apartments and range upward to $172 to $178 for two-bedroom units. If a tenant's income exceeds FHA standards, he must pay the market rate, which ranges up to $225 per month for two-bedroom units.

The management estimates that 75 percent of the current occupants are eligible for subsidies, that 20 percent pay the basic rents, and that 5 percent pay market rates. It should be noted that the so called basic rents even without subsidy are considerably below present-day market values.

20-15   MANAGEMENT

The management of the project is headed by Jan Rose, the Indianapolis representative of the Federal Property Management Corporation of Dayton, Ohio.

The first full year of operating income and expense is shown in Table 20-8. The income does not reflect the 10.6 percent increase in rent that was granted at the end of the year.

TABLE 20-8   WEYERBACHER, 12 MONTHS ENDING DECEMBER 31, 1977

	Actual	Budget	Variance
Income	$531,500	$528,000	+3,500
Expenses:			
Advertising and renting	500	600	
Minibus	3,400	3,400	
Administrative	62,400	53,400	+9,000
Electricity	83,500	70,000	+13,500
Gas	18,800	14,000	+4,800
Water	8,200	6,000	+2,200
Security	13,300	14,800	+1,500
Other operating	2,100	12,300	−12,200
Maintenance	57,000	41,000	+16,000
Other	600	600	
Total	$249,900	$216,100	+33,800
Cash flow from operations	$281,600	$311,900	−30,300
Annual debt service and escrows	254,700	266,700	−12,000
Net cash flow	$26,900	$45,200	−18,300

INDEX